THE LITTLE BLUE LIGHT

BOOKS BY EDMUND WILSON

The Little Blue Light

A PLAY IN THREE ACTS

BY

EDMUND WILSON

———————

FARRAR, STRAUS AND GIROUX
NEW YORK

First Printing, May 1950
Second Printing, (before publication) May 1950
ISBN 0-374-52666-4

Manufactured in the U.S.A. by H. Wolff Book Mfg. Co., Inc.

Designed by Stefan Salter

CHARACTERS

FRANK

JUDITH

GANDERSHEIM

ELLIS

THE GARDENER

Act One

ACT I

The back lawn of a country house about an hour and a half by train from New York. It is a late mid-September afternoon in some year of the not-remote future. One corner of the house is visible at the extreme left of the stage, revealing it as one of those monumental but clumsily-planned piles that were popular in America in the eighties. A porch runs around both sides, heavily screened by vines, with a short flight of steps that leads down to the lawn from the side that faces the audience, in such a way that it is seen sideways from the front of the stage. Above the porch, on the second floor, on the side that fills the left side of the stage, is a bow-window that swells out in a lump from the yellow wooden surface of the house. At the right of the stage, a wall, too high for passersby to see over, shuts the garden in from the public road. There is a door in the middle of this wall, against which China roses are blooming. High lilac bushes close in the back of the stage. In the middle of the lawn are four chairs and a little round table, all made of forged iron and painted white: two of the chairs are the upright kind and the others low lounging-chairs with wheels on the back legs. They are arranged around the table, the upright chairs facing the audience and the other two drawn up on either side.

A gardener, old and stooping and with longish hair, is standing, with his back to the audience, trimming a rambler vine on the side of the porch that faces it.

A woman comes out from the porch and starts down the steps but stops halfway. She is a handsome brunette, in her early thirties, but got up in such a way as not to bring out her feminine attractiveness. She wears a kind of brown business suit with a buttoned jacket, and her hair, parted straight in the middle, has been tightly stretched back and done up in a bun. She is tense, with an habitual tensity that never completely relaxes.

JUDITH. I thought that they were going to be beautiful when they bloomed the second time, those roses. The rose bugs messed them up in the summer, and I'd been hoping they'd be perfect this fall—but they're obviously going to pieces without ever having amounted to anything. They're stunted! I don't want to go near them! Nothing I have is ever right! Why can't I have flowers like other people?

THE GARDENER (*presenting himself readily and speaking eagerly, a little overacting his part*). Dey're not in de fulla bloom, *signora.*

JUDITH (*looking around*). Aren't they?

THE GARDENER (*coming forward*). You wait—you will see: in a day or two, they will be *molto belle, bellissime!* —Come and look. (*She comes down the steps and follows him over to the rose-bushes.*) See: de leetla mossa rose, she just begin to open wide.

JUDITH. You're sure they're really going to pan out?

THE GARDENER. Of course, dey panna out, *signora*— letta me showa you de Golden Dawn.

JUDITH. That name is so mushy!

THE GARDENER (*exhibiting a rose*). *Eccola, graziosa signora:* just lika de morning sky before de sun showa himself: all yellow wit' just a pale pinka flush.

JUDITH (*looking at another blossom above it*). There's something the matter with this one.

THE GARDENER (*nipping it off with his shears*). You know what maka dat, *signora?* A leetla spider—so small you can hardly see him. He eata up all de juice of de rose, and by-and-by she turna brown.

JUDITH (*as if to herself*). I don't like to hear about things like that.—I knew there was something wrong. (*She looks at the roses with distaste and apprehension.*)

THE GARDENER. Dat's de only one dat hava dat.—You wanta me to picka you some?

JUDITH. It's not too soon? Suppose they just die when I get them in the house in a vase?

THE GARDENER. Don't be afraid, *signora*. (*He begins clipping them off.*) For dem it is right now de besta moment. (*Showing her one.*) *Ecco.* It is for de roses just lika for de udder tings: if you tasta de besta moment, it lasta you all de life—if you don't tasta, de moment never come!

JUDITH. I have to have things absolutely perfect—otherwise I can't enjoy them.

THE GARDENER. *Corpo di Bacco, signora!* Nutting in all de world is absolutely perfect by itself. We must not expecta God to give us de perfect tings ready made to enjoy, to admire, to love. We must maka de life perfect by bringing to it de love and de art.

JUDITH. But if they've got spiders in them, they'll just turn brown and horrible, anyway.

THE GARDENER (*holding up a flower*). Look here: dissa rose is notta perfect—but if you wear it lika dis (*holding it against his coat*) and putta de badda part behind, you will maka de perfect rose. (*He offers it to her.*)

JUDITH (*refusing to take it*). No, I don't want it: it's blemished.

THE GARDENER. *Ah, porco Iddio, signora!* to maka de beauty from de materials dat are damaged, dat is de greatest triumph for de man.

JUDITH (*taking the roses from him*). I'll just take the good ones—thank you.—You might paint the chairs and things now that we don't use them so much. They look terrible. And I must get some cushions for the big ones! They're not comfortable a bit like that. They've been making me absolutely miserable!

THE GARDENER. Ah, *signora*, it's not de cushions dat cura de misery—it's de happiness dat maka de comfort.

JUDITH. You ought to write those moralizings down.

THE GARDENER. *Grazia, signora.*

6

JUDITH. They mightn't sound so sententious on paper.

THE GARDENER. *Scusi, signora.*

The door in the wall opens, and a gentleman appears. He is a man in his early forties, pasty and partly bald, dressed dandiacally but in rather bad taste. He wears a light gray suit, with spats, a dark green Homburg hat, a violet tie on a lighter purple shirt and a handkerchief to match sticking out of his breastpocket. He carries a light cane.

THE VISITOR (*taking off his hat*). Please pardon me for coming in like this. Is this Mrs. Brock?

JUDITH. Yes.

THE VISITOR. Well, I'm the person you're renting this house from.

JUDITH. The agent?

THE VISITOR. No: the owner.

JUDITH. M. S. Ferguson?

THE VISITOR. Yes. (*Shaking hands with self-conscious urbanity.*) It's nice to meet you at last.

The Gardener, who has watched his entrance, now turns to go back to his work and as he does so faces the audience.

THE GARDENER (*winking at the audience and dropping his Italian accent*). Just a few old platitudes!

He returns to trimming the ramblers and gradually works offstage at the left.

THE VISITOR (*going on to Judith*). I hope you don't mind my appearing by the back way like this. It's so natural for me and it's shorter from the station.

JUDITH. I thought you were in Europe.

THE VISITOR. I was, but I suddenly found I couldn't stick it and I hopped a plane and came back.

JUDITH. Won't you sit down? I'm afraid that these chairs are inexcusably uncomfortable—they're supposed to have cushions.

THE VISITOR (*sitting down in the upright chair at the left and putting his hat on the table*). They're delightful! How well you've kept things up!

JUDITH (*sitting down in the other straight chair*). I've had the garden attended to. It was in very bad shape when we came.

THE VISITOR. Really?

JUDITH. Yes: absolutely a jungle. Your caretaker hadn't done anything about it—so we got a regular gardener.

THE VISITOR. That's strange: he worked for my parents—he knew the place well.

JUDITH. He's been working for someone else, and I don't think he did much about it here.

THE VISITOR. Oh, dear: really? Did he neglect the pigeons, too? I didn't see them as I came by the stable.

JUDITH. They had some kind of disease, and most of them died.

THE VISITOR. How heartbreaking! I wanted to keep them. They were a part of the old stable and made it still seem alive. I hope you haven't minded my insisting that it shouldn't be used as a garage.

JUDITH. We did what you suggested: we rented the garage across the road.

THE VISITOR. I was sure they'd let you have it—that place has been empty, too.—You don't keep horses?

JUDITH. No; but we've had the stable repainted.

THE VISITOR. Just a shade too bright, perhaps.

JUDITH. We tried to get the same color. In a year or so it won't look so glaring.

THE VISITOR. It had a quality, I always thought. You haven't cleaned out the stalls? (*Smiling with a shade of deprecation.*) I liked to have some oats in the mangers.

JUDITH. We haven't touched it, because you asked us not to. (*With a slight sharpness of ironical intent.*) We've even left the old manure. But the building's beginning to fall to pieces: it ought to be cleaned up and repaired. It's all full of rats and things.

THE VISITOR. I don't mind rats, you know. What other things?

JUDITH. Well, thousand-leggers.

THE VISITOR. Oh, they're harmless.

JUDITH. The rats aren't, though.

THE VISITOR. You didn't poison the pigeons, I hope, in trying to poison the rats.

JUDITH. The pigeons were sick when we came. We got a bird doctor specially for them. It certainly wasn't our fault.

THE VISITOR. Don't think that I'm complaining, please. Everything that I've seen looks splendidly. One never knows what to expect of tenants, and I'd never even met you, you know.

JUDITH. So you came out to check.

THE VISITOR. I just wanted to meet you and see the place and find out how you were getting along.

9

JUDITH. My husband's reading proofs. In a few minutes, I'll let him know you're here.

THE VISITOR. Don't disturb him! I just dropped in.

JUDITH. He'll be free.—I wish you would tell me about Europe. Is the situation really worse?

THE VISITOR. Not exactly worse, perhaps, but you get to feel it more if you stay there a long time.

JUDITH. There's still not much food or coal?

THE VISITOR. Oh, there's plenty of food in the good hotels and they manage to heat them more or less. It's the atmosphere—the whole state of mind.

JUDITH. Pretty tense?

THE VISITOR. Not only tense but inhuman, in a very disconcerting way. One used to feel here in America that the people were becoming dehumanized—with all the offices and factories and subways—but now in Europe, in a different way, they're losing their individuality. You remember how they used always to be fighting for their various national cultures? The Frenchman wanted to be a Frenchman; the Czech wanted to be a Czech; the inhabitants of every little province wanted to keep their own traditions, if it merely meant putting on some old peasant dress and celebrating a local feastday. Well, the only thing they struggle for now is to perpetuate some system of slavery that is going to make them all alike. One feels that they're just clustering like iron filings on these big concentrations of power.

JUDITH. In the countries we dominate, too?

THE VISITOR (smiling ironically). In the countries the United States dominates, we've gotten ourselves into the position of backing reactionary movements that are using all the methods of fascism. I'm a conservative, but the kind of thing we're doing over there is absolutely un-American. We began by fighting the Reds, but we don't realize that their enemies are just as undesirable as they are. We've never understood Europe—at least our worthy presidents never do—and the result is that we're now being swept along by the hideous subhuman power that's wreaking havoc all over the world.

JUDITH. What power do you mean?

THE VISITOR (*as if his answer were more or less self-evident and revealing a touch of madness which makes Judith look around at him*). Why, the demiurge that's running amuck, devouring civilization.

JUDITH. Do you identify him with anything in particular?

THE VISITOR. I identify him with almost everything!

JUDITH. Oh. (*After a moment's pause.*) Has your demiurge got a name?

THE VISITOR. He's got a thousand names—you've heard them: Belial, Moloch, Kali—call him Nobodaddy, like Blake—call it the Second Coming, like Yeats, with a wild beast instead of a savior—call him Shidnats Slyme, the Monster God.

JUDITH. You're a Gandersheim addict, I see.

THE VISITOR. Well, not precisely an addict—though I know his work pretty well.

JUDITH. If you can read him at all, you're an addict. I'm one of the people that *can't* read him, but my husband is crazy about him.

11

THE VISITOR. I suppose I must make a confession so that we shan't go on talking on a false assumption. I *am* Gandersheim.

JUDITH. You're not really? I knew it was a pseudonym, but you're not like the descriptions of him.

GANDERSHEIM (*grinning slyly*). That's just our publicity—a mystification!

JUDITH. The photographs are hoaxes, too?

GANDERSHEIM. Yes: I got a friend of mine to pose.

JUDITH (*looking over to study him*). But I see that you *are* like him in some ways. Are those the violet eyes that sometimes fade to the invisible color of ultra-violet rays?

GANDERSHEIM (*rather pleased*). Perhaps.

JUDITH. And you're wearing a violet tie.

GANDERSHEIM. There are certain points, I think, where he and I fuse with one another.

JUDITH. But where's the Brazilian butterfly that you're supposed to wear in your buttonhole? and the mystic rings of priceless old jade?

(*He holds out his left hand, on one finger of which is a large jade ring.*)

GANDERSHEIM. And I do happen to know something about butterflies.

JUDITH. Is it true that you drink nothing but Armagnac from the cellar of the Comte de Germain?

Frank Brock comes down the steps from the porch. He is a loose rangy man of forty-three, dressed in a business suit of something less than the best urban cut and with longish and undisciplined hair. He wears spec-

12

tacles with dark rims and a wide razzle-dazzle tie. He is carrying the afternoon paper.

GANDERSHEIM. That's mythical, I'm afraid—but I *have* had some rather choice Armagnac. It has a flavor of violets, you see—violet and beyond, again.

JUDITH. Here's my husband.

Gandersheim gets up.

JUDITH (*to Frank*). Who do you think this is?

FRANK (*apprehensively, stopping in his tracks as he looks at Gandersheim*). I haven't the slightest idea. (*He has a rich Middle-Western voice and an emphatic Middle-Western way of talking.*)

JUDITH. Gansvoort von Gandersheim.

FRANK (*after a moment of sizing up Gandersheim and deciding it is not a joke*). No! (*Coming over and shaking hands.*) Say, I'm a fan of yours!

JUDITH. Frank used to subscribe to *Gruesome Tales* just to read the Shidnats Slyme stories.

FRANK. And now the goddam *Metropolitan*—which is otherwise a lousy magazine!

GANDERSHEIM. I'm also, under my other name, the person that you're renting this house from.

FRANK. The hell you are!

GANDERSHEIM. I just dropped in to see how you were getting on.

FRANK. Sit down! (*He throws himself into the lounging-chair on the left, as Gandersheim resumes his seat.*) Well, for goodness' sake!—and I never knew about it!

GANDERSHEIM (*pleased*). I always use my real family name, of course, in connection with personal business.

FRANK. Say, tell me: what happened to that chemistry professor when he finally got hold of the formula so that he could summon up Shidnats at will? Was he so scared by what happened the first time that he never tried it again or did he turn the demons loose on that academic cabal that was trying to block his promotion?

GANDERSHEIM. Ah, that story hasn't been written, and I'm not sure that I can give you an answer.

FRANK. I don't want to ask indiscreet questions—

GANDERSHEIM (*smiling*). Oh, it isn't a question of that. My contract with *Metropolitan's* run out, and I'm not sure they want any more stories—so I really haven't thought about what happened next.

FRANK. I don't know how I can bear it if you don't go on. I want to know whether the Shidnats adepts were able to utilize his power without blowing out their fuses.

GANDERSHEIM. It *is* rather risky, of course—it's probably safer to let it alone.

JUDITH. Mr. Gandersheim thinks that his demiurge is the dominating influence in Europe.

FRANK. I shouldn't wonder if you were right at that.

GANDERSHEIM. You know there *have* been some rather odd coincidences between certain incidents in the stories and some of the things that have been happening lately.

FRANK. What's an example?

GANDERSHEIM. Did you happen to see one of my tales called *The Octagon Building Conspiracy*?

FRANK (*nodding*). About the Shidnats cult in the war.

GANDERSHEIM. That came out before the spy revelations.

FRANK. Yes, by God, it did!

GANDERSHEIM. I sometimes have a queer kind of insight. It came to me almost like a vision. I had no private information, but one day I conceived the idea of young scientists and government officials—absolutely the conscientious type, the kind of people one would never suspect—falling under some sinister influence and betraying their country to a foreign power. It was incredible and yet it happened. And my stories usually pass for fantasy!

FRANK. That's right! The way things are getting, it's actually easier to swallow your goblins than a lot of the real stuff that's happening. That's the reason you go over the way you do: you feed the customers horror in homeopathic doses so that they're able to face the things that are going on and that keep going *on and on,* and that they can't seem to do anything about or even begin to grasp. Your shudder stories deal more or less with the same elements of murder and espionage, but the reader can get through one in three-quarters of an hour and everything is perfectly logical and leads to a satisfactory wind-up.

GANDERSHEIM. It's gratifying to hear you say that. I've always felt my work was modern.

JUDITH. With a good allowance of old-fashioned Gothic.

GANDERSHEIM. Alas, for the Gothic! It's done for, I'm afraid. One misses it in post-war Europe. There are more ruins, of course, than ever, and one can't say they aren't sometimes grisly, but it is hard to attune oneself to the older reverberations. Germany today is a limbo, full of beings that have never been really born—they're such gibbering specters themselves that they make the Wild Huntsmen and the Lenore bridegrooms seem as solid in retrospect as the old beer and pumpernickel.

JUDITH. But Italy's still romantic?

GANDERSHEIM. The landscape but not the life. There's plenty of crime, to be sure—sometimes ferocious enough —but it's mostly quite wholesale and sordid: just a routine slaughter of hostages. Nothing could be more remote from the magnificent outrages of the Borgias and the gamier days of the Papacy. In England, the big country houses that have always been so marvellously haunted are being turned by the wretched Labourites into administrative centers. Last summer I went to Glen Murtagh Castle, the Earl of Medard's place—which I've always wanted to see: it's supposed to have had a Man in Armor, a charming Woman in White and a recurrent hereditary monster—and what did I find but a rationing bureau! When I asked about the current monster, I was told by a horrid little clerk—obviously lower middle class—that it had been sent by the Earl to America to get it away from the Blitz and that "we"—meaning the Labour people—had decided not to bring it back.

JUDITH. How pathetic to be robbed of one's monsters!

GANDERSHEIM. Oh, there are monsters enough—and the new thing, of course, has its own kind of beauty. There *is* a real thrill in destruction—and destruction has never been achieved on such a gigantic scale and so completely without inhibitions. The godlike irresponsibility of it!—you're sitting up there in the clouds and (*illustrating by snapping his fingers*) you just go click, click,

click! and you pulverize whole cities—men and women and children are crushed or cooked to death, and palaces and public buildings—the big shells that they put up for show, the pedestals to make themselves important —they're all flapped away in great sheets of flame, along with the poor man's hovel and the shop that sells fish and chips—while the bomber sails along overhead as nonchalant and unremorseful as if he'd just lit up an autumn bonfire. And (*smiling*) there *were* some wonderful touches!—the tigers and snakes and apes that were let loose when the zoos were bombed and went wandering about the streets! (*Judith gives him a sharp look.*) But when one comes to it a few years later, the results do seem rather bleak. A house that's been shattered by bombing shows nothing but naked plaster—the rooms don't preserve their bad memories as a rugged old castle does—unless, of course, it happens to be a room where people have been shot against the wall or a torture chamber stained with blood. But even with a place of that sort it would take at least fifty years to make it glamorous with a patina of legend—and in the meantime it may be rebuilt—or destroyed by another blast.

JUDITH. I can see you found it very disappointing.

GANDERSHEIM. It's quite creepy enough in other ways. I was quite unnerved when I left. One day I started talking to a man on the train—I couldn't make out his nationality: he spoke English with some sort of accent—and he turned out to have read my books. I thought he knew them a little too well—as if he might just have got the subject up. It occurred to me that he might be a spy—

FRANK. Why would anybody want to spy on you?

GANDERSHEIM. I'd been expressing myself rather freely about what was going on in Europe; and it made me a little nervous when this fellow asked where I was staying—I was on my way to Florence—and said that he was stopping at the same hotel. When I got off the train in Florence, I didn't even leave the station but got right into the next train for Switzerland. But then, lo and behold! in Zürich, I hadn't been there three days before a woman turned up at my pension—a woman with an obvious wig, another creature of indeterminate nationality—who had also, it appeared, read my writings. As I always use my real name in travelling, it seemed to me rather odd that they should both have brought up my books—

FRANK (*grinning*). You're just world-famous, that's all. It's what I tell you: a lot of people have read you because they've got the same jitters you have.

GANDERSHEIM. Well, in any case, Europe was getting me down—I had a night of abject panic, and then I jumped on a plane for home. And very happy I am to be back, I can tell you!

FRANK. How long have you been away?

GANDERSHEIM. I went over the second spring after the end of the war.

FRANK. Well, I hate to hand you a wet blanket the moment you get off the boat, but you don't want to have any illusions about the kind of U.S.A. you've come back to!

18

GANDERSHEIM. You sound frightening. What do you mean? It's true I'm rather out of touch.

FRANK. Don't imagine that we haven't got plenty of spies!

GANDERSHEIM. Hardly on the same scale, surely!

FRANK. I don't know: it seems to me nowadays that every other person I see is some kind of goddam agent!—

GANDERSHEIM. But what is it they're agents of?

FRANK. Why, of all these damn pressure groups!— the same thing you have in Europe, only not operating quite so openly.

GANDERSHEIM. How disquieting!

FRANK. It's gotten to the point where I can hardly get my magazine out. I'm constantly pursued and persecuted by the lobbyists of all these groups, these various political and religious organizations, and more than half the time they're under cover.

GANDERSHEIM. I didn't realize that *Spotlight* dealt with controversial subjects.

FRANK. Hell, fifteen years ago it wouldn't have been called controversial, but today, good God! it takes all a man's strength to stand up for an independent factual article that doesn't even try to draw any conclusions!

GANDERSHEIM. But how can that be?

FRANK. It can be because what used to be everybody's privilege, that Americans took for granted—free press and free speech—has now gotten to be nothing short of a heroic individual exploit.

GANDERSHEIM. But the Bill of Rights still stands, doesn't it?

FRANK. It's still in the Constitution, but everybody wants to ignore it.

GANDERSHEIM. The radicals and the reactionaries, you mean?

FRANK. That line-up is obsolete now.

GANDERSHEIM. I do wish you'd fill me in. I'm quite ignorant about what's been happening. I couldn't make anything of the political news when I read it in The Paris *Herald.*

FRANK. It certainly isn't the politics you knew, if you left as long ago as that, and you may have some pretty severe shocks in store for you. The most important fact of the last ten years—that you'll have to begin by grasping—is the virtual disappearance of the old two-party system. What happened first of all, beginning with the New Deal, was that the Democrats swallowed everything; but by that time the Democratic Party was a collection of special interests that were competing with one another like hell—so that it got to be simply a question of which kind of Democrat you were going to elect. What it finally came down to was a scrimmage of a whole lot of organized groups, each trying to get control of the government and resorting to every kind of skulduggery—bribery, blackmail, violence—to get themselves into office.

GANDERSHEIM. But what are they?—the Reds, I suppose—but what other groups have we here?

FRANK. Well, I'll give you the political picture—reading from Right to Left. First of all, you have the Reds—they're the extreme Right: they want to institute state slavery, abolish civil rights altogether and have the coun-

try run by an oligarchy. Then you have the New Federalists—they want to restrict the vote to big employers
of labor and incomes in the upper brackets. Next come
the Constitutionalists, who are the nearest thing we've
got to a Left: they want to keep the Constitution. All
of these have political programs—they're the only big
groups that do. But that doesn't tell the whole story,
because there are all the other groups that function without programs but work for their group interests. The
strongest one now is Labor. The politicos try to exploit
it, but usually it exploits them. Then there are the
Children of Peter, with their religious organization
behind them. Actually the objectives of the Peters are
just about the same as the Reds', and their methods are
about the same. The only difference is that they're
directed from Madrid, not Belgrade, and that they make
use of a different mythology. Their principal instruments
are father confessors instead of third-degree police. But
both the Reds and the Children of Peter want to get rid
of education and to keep the working class down. They
both organize their own unions as an obstruction to the
legitimate unions that are fighting for the interests of
Labor. Last and most disgusting perhaps is the new group
of Yankee Elitists, our indigenous variety of fascists.
They're mostly just small-time snobs with the usual
careerist aspirations, who go along with the Big Business
party—though, if they think they can gain anything by it,
it's not at all unusual for them to turn into Reds over-
night. They've combined with the Southern Dixiecrats,

who want to keep the Negro disfranchised in the interests of old-time Southern chivalry.

A young man appears from the house and comes over toward the group.

GANDERSHEIM. You appal me: I came back from Europe, really *warm* about the Statue of Liberty, and you tell me we're caught in the same trap!

FRANK. Well, it's not quite so bad, even so, as what's happened to the rest of the world. There are still a few Americans left who don't want to take dictation from these mass-produced power-units. (*Getting up and raising his voice in his earnestness.*) The main stimulus to the founding of the American Republic was disobedience to the King of England, and the main principle of American vitality has always been our refusal to let anybody tell us what to do. The thing that can save us today is the thing that has made us great. We've got to have the guts to think for ourselves and act on our own ideas!

GANDERSHEIM. Hear, hear! How splendidly you say it! It quite rouses my Revolutionary blood! I date from the *Mayflower,* you know. (*Judith looks at him, and he adds, smiling:*) No, but I really do!

The young man has stopped modestly at Frank's left, so as not to intrude on the group. He is Frank's secretary Ellis, an erect clean-cut fellow of twenty-six, a product of the best education, quiet and well-bred but with a perceptible tone of conscious superiority.

FRANK (*turning to Ellis*). Did you get rid of them?

ELLIS. They've left, but they're sure to be back. They insist they've got to see you personally.

FRANK. Oh, God! What's biting them now? (*To Gandersheim.*) This is just what I was telling you about! It's the Reds who have got some squawk. (*To Ellis.*) Go ahead and tell me: I want him to hear.

ELLIS. It's that piece about the maraschino cherry-pickers. They say that our running it puts us in a class with the worst type of Yankee Elitists.

FRANK. How do they figure that out?

ELLIS. Their point is that maraschino cherries are an article of upper-class luxury—

FRANK. What's behind it?

ELLIS. What's evidently behind it is that the pickers belong to a union that's been fighting the Red infiltration.

FRANK. So what?

ELLIS. That links us with the Elitists. They serve manhattans at the Elitist banquets.

FRANK. So what?

ELLIS. They'll denounce us as Elitists and ruin our circulation among the small-income groups.

FRANK. Unless what?

ELLIS. They've left us an article setting forth the Red point of view on the crisis in the fruit-pickers' union—and they say they expect us to run it.

FRANK (*to Gandersheim*). There you are! That's what I'm up against!

JUDITH. You might introduce Ellis!

FRANK. I'm sorry. (*To Gandersheim.*) This is Ellis, my trouble-shooter. (*To Ellis.*) This is Gansvoort von Gandersheim.

ELLIS. What, really?

Gandersheim gets up and shakes hands, with a slightly Mephisophelean smile in character with his Gandersheim role.

JUDITH. Mr. Ferguson.

GANDERSHEIM. Oh, I don't mind—though of course it's a ridiculous name—a mixture of German and Knicker-bocker Dutch. I made it up when I was just a kid and signed it to the first story I ever sold.

ELLIS. I see.

JUDITH. Don't you want to sit down, Ellis?

He poises on the left arm of the other lounging-chair. Gandersheim and Frank resume their seats.

GANDERSHEIM (*to Frank*). That first story was written right here, and the name was somehow a product of the atmosphere of this queer old house.—I was rather sur-prised, by the way, that an active man of affairs like yourself should have chosen such an old-fashioned place —and so far away from New York, in such a deserted neigh-borhood.

FRANK. It was just exactly the kind of thing I was looking for. I wanted to get away from town—out of reach of these goddam propagandists.

GANDERSHEIM. But you don't direct your magazine from here?

FRANK. I absolutely do! I have an office in town, of course, where they handle the business end, but most of the editorial work is done right here in this house—done by us three!

GANDERSHEIM. Really? I'd imagined something on a bigger scale.

During the speeches of Frank that follow, Ellis and Judith, who have evidently heard all this before, talk to one another, smiling, like young people relaxing from their elders.

FRANK. Hell, you don't need a big staff if you know exactly what you want and have the self-confidence to make your own decisions. All these *(underlining the words with irony) editorial conferences* and *rewrite men* and enormous *research departments* are just ways that editors have to try to make themselves feel important because they haven't got any ideas. They try to find out what the *readers'* ideas are—they're always worrying about *circulation.* —And then—when they've worked out the formula for a standardized machine-made product that their readers will always take—they sit down and try to figure out how they can appeal to a still lower grade of readers without losing the original lot. The result in the long run is just the same as in radio and television: they're creating an artificial market for a mechanical mass-culture that depends on reducing the public to a lowest common denominator. You get something just as lifeless and boring as the movies were before they went bankrupt. The old yellow journalism was bad enough, but it at least had a certain vulgar gaudiness, and it was kept lively by competition. Today you get a processed commodity so completely devoid of flavor or of any emotion or meaning whatsoever that the only way you can force it on the customers is by killing the better grades of goods.

GANDERSHEIM. But *Spotlight* has not been eliminated!

FRANK. American journalism today has gotten to be just like the horsemeat that they put up in cans for dogs! —So long as they aren't given anything else, the Sealyham has to eat it just the same as the mutt.

GANDERSHEIM. But *you* give them something better.

FRANK. I do—and I've definitely proved that there still exist a whole lot of Americans who aren't satisfied with this goddam kennel food. I go on the opposite theory: I don't worry about the reader. I assume that any article that interests *me*—on any subject whatsoever—will interest a lot of other people. And I'm right!—by God, I'm right! I started out with *Spotlight* on a shoestring—it was practically a little magazine—and in four years and a half I've scared up a circulation of almost three hundred thousand. I've always maintained, and I've proved it, that there are still plenty of people in this country who like to read decent writing, who are actually famished for edible print—and I believe that there are lots of people who don't want their thinking done for them—especially by authoritarian groups that want to stamp out thought altogether!

GANDERSHEIM. It's heartening to hear you say so. But what is *Spotlight's* own point of view?—simply that of independent critic?

FRANK. What's our point of view, Ellis?

ELLIS. Liberalism, I suppose.

FRANK (*going on to Gandersheim*). It's not exactly

what you might think of as liberalism, though—it's something older than that. My idea is simply the old-fashioned one that everybody has a right to look at the world from the corner in which he's sitting—and to yell about anything he doesn't like.

GANDERSHEIM. So you're always treading on people's toes?

FRANK. So the various pressure publicists are always raising a howl against me—and I'm also beginning to worry the big circulation boys. It's driving them crazy to realize that there's somebody who still has the self-assurance to print whatever he pleases and who can actually make it pay. I've even swiped some of their writers, because I let them sign their names and write in their own style.

GANDERSHEIM. That's what I find so desperately annoying with the editors of *Metropolitan*: they want to rewrite all my prose.

FRANK. And what prose they put out, huh? It's like some kind of cheap cold cream!

GANDERSHEIM. But you never take sides about anything?

FRANK. I never plug a political point of view, like the liberals in the twenties did. My contention is that the abuses of the world—at least, the majority of them—have no more to do with political systems than the big acts of disinterested virtue. They're just special cases of human weakness. Take the exposé we published in the last issue. Did you ever happen to notice that when you take your watch to be mended, they always tell you it needs to be cleaned and then send it away for weeks and soak you anywhere from five to fifteen dollars? Well, the whole thing is simply a racket! Ten to one that the man you see in the store doesn't know a damn thing about watches. He doesn't have the slightest idea whether the watch is dirty or clean. He tells you anything he thinks you'll believe, sends the watch to a man who repairs them, and charges you a fanciful sum that represents what he thinks you'll pay—though the work may have taken three minutes and not be worth fifty cents.

GANDERSHEIM. How scandalous! And that, of course, has no political implications.

JUDITH. I don't agree with Frank about this.

FRANK. It's not part of an organized system! It's simply a petty swindle on the part of the watch-repairers—and there've always been petty swindles since the days of Ananias and Sapphira. I'm running a whole series of these articles, that Percy Gilman is doing—on the opticians' racket, the garage racket, the undertaking racket. Did you ever realize how the undertakers systematically exploit people's grief to make them buy fancy coffins and all kinds of unnecessary fixings?

The Gardener appears from the porch.

THE GARDENER (*to Frank*). Bertha aska me to tell you de Archbishop want to speak to you on de phone.

FRANK (*to Ellis*). What have we had about the Peters lately?

ELLIS. I don't think we've had anything for months.

FRANK. Well, see what he wants, will you? (*Ellis starts toward the house.*) Tell him I'm out of town!

FRANK (*to Gandersheim*). You can be sure he's got some gripe about something!

THE GARDENER (*to Judith*). You wanta me to mova de hydrangeas?

JUDITH (*to Gandersheim*). I really ought to consult *you* about this.

GANDERSHEIM. You thought of doing something with the hydrangeas?

JUDITH. I'd thought of moving them back near the stable.

Frank looks at the first page of his paper.

FRANK. Well, I'm damned! (*He reads an article with concentrated attention, presently turning the pages to get at the continuation.*)

GANDERSHEIM. You don't like them on the front drive?

JUDITH. They're so badly discolored. If they're meant to be blue, I'm afraid they've degenerated. They're all sort of greenish and spotty.

GANDERSHEIM. Oh, you have to put iron in the soil. They used to be very handsome.

JUDITH. I don't know what to do about them.

GANDERSHEIM. But your man here does, I'm sure. (*To the Gardener.*) *Sei italiano?*

THE GARDENER. *Parlo italiano, signore.*

GANDERSHEIM (*to Judith*). You're fortunate. They make marvellous gardeners. (*To the Gardener.*) *Di dove vieni? Da che paese?*

THE GARDENER. *Da uno paese antichissimo, signore.*

GANDERSHEIM. *Ma da quale?—dimmi. Conosco l'Italia bene.*

THE GARDENER. *Non è propriamente in Italia.*

GANDERSHEIM. *Dove dunque?*

THE GARDENER. *Non lo so più nemmeno io, signore.*

GANDERSHEIM (*to Judith*). I know Italy pretty well, but I can't identify his accent. He doesn't want to tell me where he comes from.

JUDITH. But about the hydrangeas—

GANDERSHEIM. Yes?

JUDITH. Would you mind if I moved them back?

GANDERSHEIM. Why not try to revive the color? They're very much out of fashion, I know, and some people consider them ugly, but I assure you they can be perfectly magnificent. In my mother's time, they were one of our glories: great rich round fleshy clusters that varied from blue to violet or from pink to a flushed kind of purple— and the petals had fine little veins that made them look like—like Albrecht Dürer's drawings.

JUDITH. We could work on them after we'd moved them.

GANDERSHEIM. But the approach to the house is quite fine in its way—I hope you appreciate it! Hortensias, umbrella-trees, elephant ears—all those ornamental plants of the McKinley period!—and the big silver ball in the middle.

JUDITH. We had to put the ball away.

GANDERSHEIM. Really? Why?

JUDITH. It was terribly tarnished and stained.

GANDERSHEIM. Well, one can't expect everybody to care for such things—(*nodding toward the Gardener*) I'm sure *he* understands they belong here. (*Addressing him directly*.) This place has its style, *non è vero?* though of course it's not the Boboli Gardens.

THE GARDENER. Ah, *signore,* in de Eetaly de man losa himself in de Nature; over here, when dey lay out de places like dis, dey want to maka de Nature taka de back seat.

JUDITH. There you go again!

THE GARDENER. *Scusi, signora*—all I want to say is only dat de hydrangeas and de elephant ears are justa furnishings like de silver ball, lika de Japanese vase in de hallway. It don't maka much difference if you mova dem around.

GANDERSHEIM. That's a charming and acute observation, but it does make a difference, my friend, because after all there was a pattern—a pattern that my mother worked out—and a pattern should not be spoiled. (*To Judith*.) It's astonishing the instinct they have about everything connected with aesthetics!

JUDITH (*to the Gardener*). I'll let you know later.

THE GARDENER. *Bene, signora. In ogni modo,* we could not transplanta dem dis afternoon. For de flowers it is lika for de people. You performa de operation de very first ting in de morning: den de patient have all de day to recover.

GANDERSHEIM. And a deep earthy wisdom!

JUDITH (*nodding to the Gardener*). All right.

THE GARDENER (*retiring*). *Bene, benissimo.*

FRANK (*to Judith, holding up the paper*). Look at this: another goddam political crime! Cardinal Keenan's been murdered.

31

She takes the paper from him and quickly glances through the story.

GANDERSHEIM. Political murders, too? In the old days, we shot only the presidents!

THE GARDENER (*turning away toward the audience and walking back to the house*). *Il trionfo della morte! Avanti Savoia!*

FRANK (*to Judith*). That looks like a Red job. (*To Gandersheim.*) The mystery is how they did it. He was burned to death in some way.

GANDERSHEIM. Where did they find his body?

FRANK. He was sitting at his desk in his study. It was almost as if he'd been electrocuted.

GANDERSHEIM. It's strange that electrocution hasn't been more used for murders. You can electrocute a person, you know, with as little as fifty volts and generate that much current with an equipment that can be carried in a cigar-box. Were the electrical fixtures examined?

Ellis appears from the house and comes over toward the group.

FRANK. He'd just been talking on the phone—the receiver was still in his hand, but the telephone seemed perfectly normal—the insulation was all right.

JUDITH. What about the burnt-out flashlight?

FRANK. That was on the other side of the room. —And electrocution doesn't singe the skin. The whole upper part of his body was blackened—though his clothes were only burned from the inside.

JUDITH. But you've only got the reports of the Peters.

They had a chance to set the stage. I'll bet they did it themselves, just to create a martyr!

FRANK. I don't think they'd go that far. After all, the Reds in Europe have supplied them with more martyrs than they need.

JUDITH. They haven't any over here. I wouldn't put it past them.

FRANK. It wouldn't be worth it to them. The value of martyrs has slumped. Since the air-bombings and the concentration camps and the Stalingrad holocaust, nobody but a few old cranks cares a damn about human life. Our emotional thermometer's blown its top: we don't react to those things any more. My guess is that for some special reason the Reds wanted to get rid of the Cardinal and counted on its passing as a natural death. (*To Ellis.*) What was the call about?

ELLIS. Just what you're talking about.

FRANK. The Archbishop, by God! I forgot.

ELLIS. They've arrested Percy Gilman.

FRANK. Why?

ELLIS. He's supposed to have been the last person who'd been in Keenan's study.

FRANK. What had Percy gone to see him about?

ELLIS. It seems that the undertakers got wind of the article he's doing and that the ones who work for the Peters and overcharge their customers so outrageously are protected by the church organization. They've been making big contributions to the fund for the new cathedral. Percy Gilman had gone to see the Cardinal to find out what he'd say about it.

FRANK. He *would* go off on a tangent like that! He's one of those old-fashioned liberals who are always raising political issues! —Well, what, in Heaven's name, is supposed to have happened? Is he supposed to have made Keenan so sore that he had a stroke and fell dead?

ELLIS. They accuse him of carbonizing the Cardinal with some kind of canned lightning.

JUDITH. That flashlight?

ELLIS. It seems suspicious. They can't make out how it worked.

FRANK. That's absolute idiocy! What motive is Percy supposed to have had?

ELLIS. They've dug up the fact that years ago he lost his job in one of the public schools for telling his pupils that Jefferson and Franklin were skeptics about religion. He wrote some articles at that time, it seems, against the Peteristic influence on education.

FRANK. That was way back in the forties!

ELLIS. They claim that he was going on the warpath again. They say he's a fanatic, a madman. They're making the most of the fact that he once had a nervous breakdown and was sent to a sanitarium.

FRANK. What did the Archbishop want?

ELLIS. It was his secretary. He wants you to testify that Gilman was an erratic character.

FRANK. The hell I will! He's an old New Deal hack—conscientious and low-keyed to a fault.

ELLIS. He says that the undertaking article has got to be dropped right away and that you've got to publish that series on the human side of parish Peters.

FRANK. I rejected that.

ELLIS. He wants you to reconsider it.

FRANK. What's their blackmail?

ELLIS. They'll get us suppressed.

FRANK. Incitement to violence?

ELLIS. No: under the obscenity statute.

FRANK. What have we run, for God's sake, that could possibly be called obscene?

ELLIS. That article on window-dummies.

FRANK. It says they're well-modelled, but what the hell?

ELLIS. It says they're incomplete anatomically, and they claim that amounts to indecency.

GANDERSHEIM. But surely that's perfectly preposterous! I've been reading some newsstand thrillers, and they're absolutely filthy.

The Gardener comes down the steps and crosses toward the group.

FRANK. I don't know: it's happened before. In New York, the Children of Peter can always write the court decisions, and they can rule that a pencil-sharpener's immoral.

THE GARDENER (*to Frank*). *Signore.*

FRANK (*apprehensively*). What is it now?

THE GARDENER. A phone-call for you, *signore.*

FRANK. Who is it?

THE GARDENER. A newspaper reporter. He says he work for de *Standard.*

FRANK. Tell him I've gone out to the West Coast.

THE GARDENER. *Bene, signore.*

35

ELLIS. Don't you think it might be worth while to find out what the reporter knows?

JUDITH. I'd talk to him!

The Gardener stops to see whether Frank will change his mind; but goes on when Frank begins making a speech, and disappears into the house.

FRANK. Nowadays they never know anything! You can't find out anything from reading the papers. (*He goes on holding forth to Gandersheim, while Ellis takes the newspaper from Judith and sits down in the lounging-chair to read it.*) The audacious American journalist who dashes to the center of tension and uncovers something that wasn't known is just as obsolete today as the cracker-barrel editorial-writer who thinks up his own comments. They both subsist entirely on handouts from the various publicity departments, and the only people who really know what's happening are the top inner committees of these anti-democratic groups. I've been a journalist all my life—I spent ten years as a city editor—but lately I've had to admit that I haven't got the slightest idea who's doing what to whom—and there are times when I'm not sure that I care much. They're all about equally stulti-fying!

JUDITH. So you're going to capitulate to the Peters?

FRANK. No: what in hell makes you think so?

Gandersheim, not to seem to pay attention to a conversation that shows signs of acerbity, takes the paper from Ellis, who has laid it on his knee and looked around.

JUDITH. Well, the Yankee Elitists persuaded you to

pretty much retract your statement about F. Bulfinch Boudinot.

FRANK. I'm not going to sell Percy out and I'm not going to get suppressed.

JUDITH. What do you propose to do?

ELLIS. Hadn't I better get in touch with your lawyer.

FRANK. More lawyers: my God!

JUDITH. They certainly let you down the last time.

FRANK. Don't be so defeatist.

JUDITH. I'm not defeatist: I think you ought to fight.

FRANK. Of course I'm going to fight. I'm going to take the offensive. I'm going to find out for myself for once exactly what's happened and why.

JUDITH. Who will you get to do it? You're not planning to investigate yourself?

FRANK (*ironically*). That would be a dandy idea, wouldn't it?

ELLIS. How about that little man who did the exposé of the Trotter poll?

FRANK (*to Gandersheim*). That's something you ought to know about! It turns out that when they take these polls, they don't actually make a bona fide effort to find out what people think: they're paid by various interests to manufacture public opinion by producing the right kind of predictions.—(*To Ellis.*) The fellow that wrote those articles has departed from the world of reality: he's working for a foundation now.

GANDERSHEIM (putting down the paper). It's strange that no one heard any noise. There were several other

37

people in the house. One can only imagine something like an enormous oxy-acetylene blow-torch.

FRANK (*to Ellis, announcing a sudden idea*). Do you know who's going after this story?

ELLIS. Have you got an inspiration?

FRANK. *You* are!

ELLIS. I'm afraid I can't quite see that.

FRANK (*springing to his feet again*). You're just the ideal person!

ELLIS. But wouldn't it be better to get somebody who isn't connected with the magazine?

FRANK. That doesn't make any difference. The great thing about it is that nobody will take you seriously. Don't misunderstand me, but they'll think you're a perfect ninny. You'll be obviously out of your element, and they'll think you're naïve and diffident—those professional foxes and weasels won't pay any attention to you. But the fact is—*you* know and *I* know—that you're a hell of an astute guy. You're the sharpest checker of copy and the deftest brusher-off of visitors that I've ever had working for me—and you can size up a situation as shrewdly as anybody I've ever known. What's more, you have the qualification that your father was an Episcopal minister and that you worked for the Federated Churches—

ELLIS. I was just Father's secretary.

FRANK. But you got to know the leaders in the religious world.

ELLIS. I don't exactly like to exploit the connections I made through Father.

FRANK. He's dead now, isn't he?

ELLIS. But even so.

GANDERSHEIM (*embarrassed by the conversation, in a low voice to Judith*). Do you mind if I look at the roses?

They go over to the wall together, and he comments on the various bushes, but she keeps an ear out for the others and sometimes glances in their direction.

FRANK. Well, you've lost your religious faith, you told me, and I hope you've got some faith in *Spotlight*. This is a goddam critical situation: the whole issue of a free press is at stake—and it may mean saving an innocent man. With the power that the Peters have now, they might be able to railroad Percy to the chair.

ELLIS. I can't imagine that I'm the right person; but if you really think I could be any use—

FRANK. You can if you start right away and get around before they've framed their case. Go to people in the other churches and find out where Keenan stood and who would have had an interest in killing him—then, when you know what questions to ask, go and see the big Peters.

ELLIS. I used to know Bishop Fay pretty well.

FRANK. If possible, get something on them. If they threaten us, we'll blackmail them back.

ELLIS. I shouldn't like to betray people's confidence.

FRANK. Don't worry: *they* wouldn't hesitate. The whole Peter business is a confidence game. I've always said they ought to be hauled into court under the Blue Sky Law. They take money for priorities in Purgatory when there isn't any such place.

ELLIS (*smiling*). I'm not sure I can be that hardboiled.

FRANK. It's a matter of defending the decencies against gangs that don't give a damn for them.—Now go and grab your suitcase and catch the 6:40! (*He takes out his watch and looks quickly at it.*) You've only got twenty minutes.

JUDITH (*coming back with Gandersheim*). Are you actually going, Ellis?

ELLIS (*grinning self-consciously, but with a certain boyish enjoyment*). I feel like a character in a spy story.

GANDERSHEIM. A Galahad!

FRANK (*to Ellis*). Now scram. I'll brief you on the way to the train.

Ellis strides off to the house.

GANDERSHEIM (*to Frank*). I'm absolutely thrilled by this, you know! You're a real man of action, aren't you?

FRANK. And I've got another brilliant idea! *You're going to write for Spotlight!*

GANDERSHEIM. I'm afraid I don't have any talent for exposés and that kind of thing.

FRANK. It's your stories I want, for God's sake! I've never run any fiction, but your stories are something special. If your contract with *Metropolitan* runs out and they're harassing you the way you say, why not let me publish your stuff? Whatever they've been paying you, I'll better it.

GANDERSHEIM. I'm not happy with *Metropolitan,* it's true: not only are they ruining my prose, they've been sticking me over in the back among the body-odor ads— and at the same time breaking up my stories with the

40

most impossible illustrations of athletic-looking young men and women that contradict the whole uncanny atmosphere I need to create my effects.

FRANK. Don't worry about illustrations—I promise not to put any of your hobgoblins into bathing-suits or wooden brazeers.—We'll have dinner in a minute or two and we can talk about terms afterwards.

GANDERSHEIM. Oh, I won't stay to dinner! —I just dropped in.

FRANK. Yes, you will—we'll be eating right away.

GANDERSHEIM (*looking toward Judith, as she does nothing to second the invitation*). It can't be convenient for you to have me on such short notice. I'll take the train with the young man.

FRANK (*to Judith*). Tell him to stay.

JUDITH. Yes: do stay.

GANDERSHEIM. I'd be charmed if it's really not too much trouble.

JUDITH. I'll tell Bertha. (*She goes into the house.*)

GANDERSHEIM (*to Frank*). Since you're kind enough to be interested in the Shidnats myth, you might like to know that it was first conceived right here in this very house.

FRANK. You don't say!

GANDERSHEIM (*nodding toward the second floor*). That window up there is the one through which Shidnats first appeared to Gandersheim. The original series of stories, you know, were told in the first person.

FRANK. You mean the window where the landscape

41

would change and be transformed into something unearthly?

GANDERSHEIM. Yes: the runes are carved above it. Did you notice them?

FRANK. I'll be damned—so that's what that is!

GANDERSHEIM. They're not really carved, of course. I cut them out with my jigsaw when I was just a kid. That's when the whole thing got started.

FRANK. Sit down.

Frank drops back into his lounging-chair; Gandersheim takes a seat in the straight chair at the right. The sun is setting and it begins to get dark.

GANDERSHEIM. I had rather a lonely childhood—to explain how the whole thing came about. We lived out here with very few neighbors that we particularly cared to know—this locality had already ceased to be fashionable—and I was an only child. In the summers when I was not going to school, I used to get so unspeakably bored! I'd lie up there on the window-seat and imagine that if I looked out the window at just the right moment of twilight, I'd suddenly see something different from the same old trees and fields—something exciting and troubling. Every summer we planned to travel, but we never got off on a decent trip. My mother was a professional invalid, and when the time for departure approached, she always turned out to be ill. I see now that she was a hopeless neurotic, so the whole thing could have been predicted—but every time it was the same disappointment—I used just to break down with despair when I was first told we couldn't go—and then I'd resign myself, try not to get too depressed but to keep myself keyed down to our stagnant life. I had to conjure up a new country that I could get to without leaving home—and that's how Shidnats Slyme began: Shidnats was the god of that country.

Ellis has come out of the house, carrying a small and very smart leather suitcase and wearing a summer straw-hat with a striped blue-and-black band. Judith follows behind him.

ELLIS. Well, I'm off. (*To Frank.*) I'll need some money.

FRANK (*pulling out his pocketbook*). I'll arrange for you to draw in town. (*Finding only ten dollars in his pocketbook.*) Wait a minute! (*He brings a checkbook out of the pocket of his coat and, taking a fountain-pen from his breast-pocket, sits down at the table and writes out a check.*)

GANDERSHEIM (*to Ellis*). Do I see a St. Matthew's band?

ELLIS. Yes. It's high time I got a fall hat.

GANDERSHEIM. I went to St. Matthew's.

ELLIS. *Did* you?

GANDERSHEIM. I didn't finish, but I'm proud of having been there, and it's cheering to see that band. With so much vulgarity rampant and the ground quaking under one's feet, it's somehow reassuring to know that the old school still endures. —Were you there when Dr. Parkes was still alive?

ELLIS. No, but we heard a lot about him.

GANDERSHEIM. I had a real admiration for him. He was a really imaginative person. He had the good taste

43

not to fire me when I was caught reading a book on the Black Mass.

ELLIS. You're not Froggy Ferguson?

GANDERSHEIM. I am.

ELLIS. By my time you'd become a legend. Did you really hold rites in the lumber-room and offer up a Second-Form boy as a human sacrifice?

GANDERSHEIM (*rather pleased*). No, of course not—that's all nonsense. The worst thing we did up there was to burn a few bad-smelling chemicals.

FRANK (*handing Ellis the ten-dollar bill and the check*). Here you are. Cash this at your club.

ELLIS. Thanks.

FRANK (*looking at his watch again*). Now, let's get started.

ELLIS. OK. (*To Gandersheim, quickly shaking hands.*) Nice to have seen you. (*Saluting Judith.*) Wish me luck.

JUDITH. I do.

He and Frank go out through the gate, Frank taking him by the arm and beginning at once to instruct him.

GANDERSHEIM (*to Judith*). A splendid young chap, isn't he?—and so plucky to go off in that way! (*She is brooding and does not reply.*) St. Matthew's *does* turn out gentlemen. I'm sorry I didn't graduate. The old doctor didn't want to expel me—he didn't take my Satanism seriously; but he punished me in a crushing way that ruined my whole spring term, and my mother was so indignant that she wouldn't let me go the next year—so I only had two years. I found myself stuck here again. It was horrible, all wrong—I was too old to be at home. I

44

really got to hate poor Mother. She had a noose around everyone's neck—and when Father died and she was here alone, I knew that it was out of the question for me to think of going to college.—(*As he becomes aware that Judith is looking at him rather detachedly.*) Please forgive all this reminiscence! Coming out here has brought it back.

JUDITH. When did you get off to Europe? (*She sits down in the straight chair on the right.*)

GANDERSHEIM. Not till I was seventeen—but it probably saved me from going mad. I made Mother take me abroad and we lived two years in Florence. Then we came back to the States, so that Mother could get better medical attention, and, to everybody's surprise, she died. I'm afraid that my father had bored her to death—with his stuffy old business in Worth Street and his interest in the Civil War. He did get through the crash, though, unscathed. He left me a small steady income—and, after my parents died, I had no real ties in this country, and my great friend was living in Florence, so I went back there and stayed—till the war began making things intolerable. I'd always kept up this house. Though I'd thought, when I left it first, that I never wanted to see it again, I found, when I came back to the States, that it was the only place I really belonged.

JUDITH. I'm sorry about the pigeons.

GANDERSHEIM. Well, of course, one can't hope to save everything—especially when one isn't here. I'm delighted —quite thrilled—as a matter of fact, at finding you so *simpatico*. I always have a certain sinking, a sensation almost like panic, when I first get back to this house. It's the world of my adolescence—irresistible and yet repellent—and the horror of Shidnats Slyme always seems to be lurking for me here. He appeared to me first in this house, and (*with a deprecatory smile*) I still expect to find him in residence. He embodies himself sometimes in people, pretends to be a human being, but I always recognize his presence. I was telling you about my experience in Europe—my horrible qualms in that pension. And I felt a slight touch of it today when I was coming out here to see you. After all, what did I know about your husband! The editor of a popular magazine—that might mean the Monster God! Why should such a man bury himself in a remote abandoned place like this unless he were an adept of the cult—or even an incarnation?—

Frank comes back through the gate.

GANDERSHEIM. I was just telling your wife that this house has a peculiar emotional effect on me: I can't get over the notion that Shidnats is somewhere around.

FRANK. Well, I haven't seen that noisome green liquid oozing out from under any of the doors—though we've had some serious trouble with the plumbing.

GANDERSHEIM. *You* keep him away! You're the power that works against him—the power that works for good. I was just telling your wife how happy I was to find such a man in possession: an unterrified champion of all the things that Americans have got to keep if they're going to hold their heads up—a warrior who is fighting *my* battles!

FRANK (*not displeased but cutting him short*). Everybody's got to fight!—Do you want to wash before dinner?

GANDERSHEIM. If I might.

FRANK. There's a bathroom at the left, right inside that door.

GANDERSHEIM (*smiling*). I know where the bathrooms are.

FRANK (*grinning*). Sorry: this business has distracted my mind. I forgot that you were in your own house.

GANDERSHEIM. I have a peculiar reason for remembering that first-floor bathroom!

FRANK. Was it a hideout for Shidnats Slyme?

Gandersheim gives a coy and eerie laugh and goes up the steps to the house.

FRANK (*to Judith*). By God, I'm inspired today! There was a moment when I thought it was getting me down, but then I made a big comeback!

JUDITH. *I* think you're making a mistake.

FRANK. About sending Ellis?

JUDITH. Yes—about that Gandersheim, too.

FRANK. I know you don't like his stuff—

JUDITH. He's screwy. He was going on just now in a perfectly loony way. He's got delusions of persecution.

FRANK. He's eccentric—nothing worse, I'd say.

JUDITH. You'll alienate your serious readers by printing that rubbish of his. You might just as well run a comic-strip!

FRANK. If *I* like it, why shouldn't *they*? I consider him a top-notch asset. His following's been growing steadily. There's no question about it: at the present time, he's America's Number One bugaboo-monger.

JUDITH. And Ellis isn't going to be able to do what you want him to do.

FRANK. I've got a lot of confidence in him.

JUDITH. But he just isn't brash enough to walk in where he's not wanted, and he's too reserved himself to make people tell him things.

FRANK. He's all steamed up about it—he's just boyish enough to enjoy it. He's smart and he's got no commitments—and his innocence is his great advantage. He'll be able to see the goddam obvious things that there's a general conspiracy not to see.

JUDITH. In the meantime, I suppose you realize that I'll have to interview all the people and take all the telephone calls.

FRANK. I'll get somebody out from the office.

JUDITH. No, you won't: you'll decide as usual that there's nobody there that can handle it.

FRANK. Don't worry: you won't have to do it.

JUDITH. *I* think it would be a lot better if you'd attend to some of those things yourself.

FRANK. Where would I get the time?

JUDITH. After all, you don't have to read proof—and it makes a bad impression on people never to be willing to see them. You seem to yourself so courageous, but you're getting the reputation of always evading and hiding—and I don't feel that I can take it again to be the person you hide behind.

FRANK. You won't have to: you can go on gardening.

JUDITH. You know that I'm no good at gardening—that old man does it all—and Gandersheim has done nothing

48

but complain that things aren't the way they ought to be.

FRANK. Well, you won't have to do Ellis's work. That's that!

JUDITH. Not that I've got anything better to do. I'm sure I don't know what you think there is in this kind of life for *me*—I can tell you there isn't much.

FRANK. What's the matter? This sounds like last winter. I thought you'd been liking it here lately.

JUDITH. I *was.*

FRANK. Well, what's wrong now? Tell me.

JUDITH. It's just that you're so completely inconsiderate when you begin throwing your weight around.

FRANK. How many times do you want me to tell you that I'm going to get another secretary?

JUDITH. It isn't only that. I was just getting everything organized, and now you've sent Ellis away and spoiled it.

FRANK. It isn't as if he wasn't coming back.

JUDITH. I'd planned that party for Friday.

FRANK. Well, what's to prevent your having it?

JUDITH. I counted on Ellis for tennis.

FRANK. I'll play, what the hell!

JUDITH. No: you're terrible. Nobody wants to play doubles with you.

FRANK (*morosely, an idea dawning*). You're going to miss Ellis a lot?

JUDITH. Of course I am.

FRANK. I see.

The dinner gong is sounded. She starts for the house.

FRANK (*following her*). I didn't know you liked him

49

that much. You were telling me he was too conventional.

JUDITH. I've gotten to like him very much.

FRANK. Oh, God: another crush!

JUDITH. You know that I like Ellis and you sent him away on purpose.

FRANK. I swear I never gave it a thought!

JUDITH. It's your absolutely psychopathic jealousy—you don't want me to have any friends!

They go up the steps, she first.

FRANK. Oh, don't start that!

JUDITH. It's instinctive with you to cut me off from everybody I like.

FRANK. We'll talk about this later.

JUDITH. No, we won't!

She goes into the house, and he follows.

Act Two

*Mid-October: half past five in the afternoon. The work-
room on the second floor of Gandersheim's house, in
which Frank and Judith are living. This was formerly
an upstairs library but has been converted into a sort of
editorial office (Frank has his own study on the floor below), and now contains an incongruous mixture of the
original library furniture with modern office equipment.
The walls are panelled in dark stained oak in the style
of the early nineteen hundreds. On the right, toward the
front of the stage, the big bow-window, which was seen
from the ouside in Act I, makes a recess with a wide
cushioned window-seat, and the audience have a glimpse
of the panes, with the frieze of jigsaw "runes" above them,
but they cannot see out the window. In the middle of
the back wall is a fireplace with a carved wooden mantelpiece, on which stands a clock surmounted by a small
bronze figure and above which hangs a large steel en-*

53

graving: the well-known nineteenth century group called Shakespeare and His Friends. *On either side of the fireplace are bookcases that rise somewhat higher, in which the old leather-bound sets have partly been replaced by up-to-date reference books. One bookcase is ornamented with a large stuffed owl, the other with a terrestrial globe. There is a morris-chair, with a floor lamp beside it, in the corner to the right of the fireplace. In the lefthand corner, against the left wall, is an old mahogany desk, with a flap that comes down on hinges. It is open: there is a typewriter on it and a highbacked chair in front of it. Further forward along this left wall are a row of steel filing-cases and above them a bulletin board on which are tacked up schedules for coming issues of* Spotlight, *lists of articles or ideas for articles, etc. Further forward, there is a door that leads into the hall and opens toward the front of the stage so that the audience can see the doorway as soon as the door is opened. Stretching across the middle of the room, parallel with the back wall and further back than the bow-window, stands a long plain unfinished table, on which are papers, pencils, pen and ink, ashtrays and cigarettes, newspapers and magazines and two green-shaded student-lamps, and around which are grouped several chairs. One of these, at the right-hand end, is the mate to the highbacked chair at the desk: the others are miscellaneous—some of them old-fashioned, with cushioned seats, others office furniture, hard and stiff.*

Judith, in harlequin glasses, a plain but smart working suit and a man's shirt with a necktie and a buttoned-down collar, is sitting in the highbacked chair, at the end of the long table, editing a manuscript with an evidently ruthless hand.

Ellis opens the door and comes in, leaving the door half open. He is carrying a briefcase, which he lays on the table.

JUDITH. Oh, hello! (*She takes off her glasses.*)

ELLIS. You stood me up again.

JUDITH. I'm sorry. I missed the nine forty-five, because Frank had taken the car—as usual, without telling me—and then I couldn't get anybody to wait on me in that new Park Avenue place where they have those men's clothes for women—the sales girls are getting so snooty that they don't want to sell you anything—and then the taxi-driver took me West instead of East before I noticed where we were going—it may have been my fault: he said I told him West but I was sure I told him East. When I got to the Tally-Ho, you'd gone.

ELLIS. I couldn't wait: I had an appointment with the head of the Constitutionalist Committee.

JUDITH. I called you up, but you weren't there—then I didn't want to call from here.

ELLIS. Why? On account of Frank?

JUDITH. I'd told him I was lunching with you, and it wasn't very well-received.

ELLIS. Really?

JUDITH. Have you seen him?

ELLIS. Just for a minute. He said he was busy.

JUDITH. Was he nasty?

ELLIS. The same as usual.

JUDITH. He's never very gracious, is he?

ELLIS. He's all right. They tell me that newspaper men are all more or less like that.

JUDITH. He's really full of hate.

ELLIS. Why?

JUDITH. Because he never was the newspaper man he wanted to be. He doesn't know he's frustrated, though, because he's too extraverted. He doesn't even know he's extraverted.

ELLIS. Isn't that all right for a journalist?—to throw himself out into public events?

JUDITH. Frank doesn't throw himself out, though— he's always hiding away. He always makes somebody else grapple with the actual problems—you, for instance.

ELLIS. And I've been no good.

JUDITH. Nothing new?

ELLIS. Not a thing. (*He sits down in a chair near the middle of the table, on the side that faces the audience.*) What I hear from the Consties is that the Reds and the New Federalists and the Dixiecrats and the Children of Peter have all made a deal for the election. They think they're going to have a tough time to prevent a Constitutionalist victory. So nobody will talk about the murder or any delicate matter of that kind. It's really the most amazing thing how well-disciplined these movements are. Even the high-school children: if you mention any public issue, they'll reel off the latest directive as if it were Boyle's law of gases. The difference is, though, that a scientific law remains the same from year to year whereas their directives are always changing—and I suppose they grow up to believe that the truth is always changing—in other words, that the truth is something that has no connection with reality.

JUDITH. What about that ex-Red, that newspaper man, who told you he'd known about it?

ELLIS. He turned out to be a spy for the Peters.

JUDITH. Yes: I never believed that story.

ELLIS. It's a good thing we published it, though. The Peters were all ready to have us suppressed—I just found that out for certain.—Otherwise, I've been a flop.

JUDITH. No, you haven't. Frank was just saying that for the first time you'd made him "see the picture," as he calls it.

ELLIS. He gave me a bawling-out on the phone the other day.

JUDITH. Don't take it from him. Just snap back at him, and you'll find he'll always recoil.

ELLIS. I'm not quite in a position to do that.—How's Gandersheim working out as secretary?

JUDITH. Frank thinks he's wonderful, but I think he's dreadful.

ELLIS. A little on the spooky side.

JUDITH. What I really can't stand is that he's making this place a headquarters for his nauseating brotherhood. He has hundreds of fans, it seems. He writes to them on paper with a phony crest, and they come out here to talk poltergeists with him. The truth is that Gandersheim's myth is a literary power cult—for armchair romantics and second-rate pansies.

ELLIS. I'd imagined that Shidnats Slyme was presented as a monstrous menace.

JUDITH. The attitude toward him is ambivalent.

ELLIS. I haven't heard that word for ages. In the forties people used it all the time.

JUDITH. It was indispensable then because it gave a certain dignity to trying to have things both ways.

ELLIS. It could also be pronounced "ambilavent."

JUDITH. And they would talk about "having a block." Are you old enough to remember that? To talk about "having a block" was a way of giving scientific standing to some humiliating deficiency—like not being able to spell—or some failure to keep some promise that you didn't want to keep.

ELLIS. That was what happened to you yesterday when you missed the train and all that.

JUDITH. I was really afraid of Frank.

ELLIS. You don't use that technique you were just recommending?

JUDITH. I didn't want a quarrel.

ELLIS. Some other day maybe?

JUDITH. Maybe.

ELLIS. How do Gandersheim's followers go down with Frank?

JUDITH. He stands for them because Gandersheim adores him. He just drools after Frank—it's sickening. But Frank thinks it's perfectly natural that people should be his abject slaves.

ELLIS. He's not taken in, though, by people, beyond a certain point.

JUDITH. I've never seen him gag at flattery.

ELLIS. Well, he's got a great deal more shrewdness—and a great deal more independence—than those mugs I've been seeing in town. All they want is to be yessed by their underlings, and then they yes their higher-ups. I have a lot of admiration for Frank.

JUDITH. Then you oughtn't to ask me to lunch.

ELLIS. I really miss you a lot.

JUDITH. You don't.

ELLIS. I've realized how much you've meant to me since I've been staying up there in town.

JUDITH. Oh, no, I haven't.—What have I meant?

ELLIS. You're the only girl I ever knew who had the same kind of brains as a man and yet at the same time was perfectly beautiful.

JUDITH. New York is full of types like me. You haven't seen the latest crop of career girls.

ELLIS. *You're* not a career girl.

JUDITH. How do you know?

ELLIS. If you were, you wouldn't be out here.

JUDITH. But I don't like being out here. This isn't really my role. Now that you're away and with Gandersheim here, this place is getting me down. I'm absolutely stuffy and stale.

ELLIS. Then meet me for a drink some day. You won't have to explain about it.

JUDITH. It's too serious when you don't explain.

ELLIS. Not necessarily, is it?

JUDITH. It seems to work out that way.

ELLIS. Not that I'm not prepared to be serious.

JUDITH. It's better the way it is. What we have is a "joking relationship." Did you ever study anthropology? They talk about "joking relationships." When a Navaho Indian, for example, meets one of his aunts on his father's side, they're supposed to exchange badinage—and I guess that a boss's wife and a husband's secretary ought to have the same kind of relationship.

ELLIS. I shouldn't think that would always be a good idea. It would produce too many bad jokes.

JUDITH. Thank you!

ELLIS. I didn't mean you. You're brilliant.

JUDITH. I'm not: I'm getting so stupid that I couldn't amuse a baby—though actually I don't like babies, I never know what to do about them.

ELLIS. You don't care for children.

JUDITH. No: not other people's! I'd like to have some boys of my own—but I wouldn't like them when they were little.

ELLIS (after a brief pause, during which he has been asking himself whether he ought to go on with the subject). Maybe children are what you need.

JUDITH. I don't know: I don't want them now.—It may be too late for me to have them.

ELLIS. Not necessarily, is it?

JUDITH. Oh, I don't know! How did we get on this subject? Let's drop it!

ELLIS. You're not sure you want to stay with Frank?

JUDITH. I suppose that's really it—though I usually give other reasons. I'm fond of Frank, of course, but it's not really right between us. He's so much older than I

60

am. I began by being his secretary, and I still can't help feeling like a secretary—a secretary who occasionally sleeps with the boss.

ELLIS. But you married him.

JUDITH. It's easier to be married if you're going to live together in the country.

Gandersheim has appeared in the doorway and stands listening to the conversation, concealed from Judith and Ellis by the partially closed door.

ELLIS. I thought that there was quite a lot more than that between you and Frank.

JUDITH. Oh, there was, I suppose, but—oh, I don't know!—I guess maybe it's just that nowadays I don't even have a woman-friend to get together with and beef about our husbands. I've felt completely flat since you left.

ELLIS (*getting up and coming over to her*). I need somebody to confide in, too—so why don't you meet me in town for a drink?—and be sure to make it this time!

JUDITH. I've been having awful migraines lately—and when they hit me, I can't do anything.

ELLIS (*smiling*). Psychosomatic, no doubt?

JUDITH. That's another great comforting word.

ELLIS. Like "that blessed word Mesopotamia" that the old woman found in the Bible.

JUDITH. Yes: of course "psychosomatic" is a mystical idea, isn't it?—Something like the Incarnation.

ELLIS. You're the brightest girl I ever knew.

JUDITH. Girl? I'm getting middle-aged.

ELLIS. Next Saturday?

JUDITH. All right.

She looks up at him, and he leans down and kisses her. They remain for a moment in silence, her mouth pressed against his.

ELLIS (*straightening up*). How about five at the Tally-Ho?

JUDITH. I'd have to make it earlier than that—I'd have to get back well before dinner.

ELLIS. Four o'clock then?

JUDITH. All right.

Gandersheim quietly enters and closes the door behind him. He has a handful of unfolded letters. Ellis looks around and sees him.

ELLIS (*to Gandersheim*). Have you been having an awful time with all that?

GANDERSHEIM. Oh, no: it comes quite easily. (*He goes over to the desk with the typewriter.*)

ELLIS. You're wonderful at the brush-off, I understand.

GANDERSHEIM. A touch of mystification helps.

JUDITH (*whose feeling of guilt and fear lest they may have been overheard leads her to propitiate Gandersheim*). He's the master of the evasive answer. He doesn't just tell them that Frank is away. He tells them something that confuses them so that they're absolutely stopped in their tracks.

ELLIS (*to Gandersheim*). How would you handle a specific case?

JUDITH. Tell him how you disposed of the Elitist.

GANDERSHEIM (*coming forward to the long table*). Oh, he was trying to pump me about Frank's politics, and I

62

told him that *Spotlight's* position was that of a floating platform stabilized between the planets in interstellar space, and that Frank's point of view was that of a celestial engineer whose problem was to keep them hanging there by maintaining a delicate balance between the various gravitational pulls.

ELLIS. Nice work. How did he take it?

GANDERSHEIM. He asked me starkly which candidate Frank would support, and I replied that the function of *Spotlight* was not to support but to scrutinize.

ELLIS. Masterly! I envy your resourcefulness.

JUDITH. Tell him about the currency crank.

GANDERSHEIM. Oh, that was quite fantastic. A wild-eyed fellow appeared who had one of these panaceas for curing our economic ills. It was a perfectly simple device: you would issue some paper money that had double denominations—that is, there would be bills, for example, that had five dollars printed on one side and ten on the other side—and anybody who could certify that his income was below a certain level could use them for the larger amount.

ELLIS. What was your flabbergasting answer?

GANDERSHEIM. I told him that, from our point of view, all value was already relative, and that to issue a two-sided currency would only make things more complicated.

ELLIS. I'm full of admiration. I never really had the right knack for dealing with the lunatic fringe.

Frank comes in.

FRANK. We're scooped!

63

ELLIS. What?

FRANK. That murder's been pinned on the Reds.

ELLIS (*getting up*). Where did you hear that?

FRANK. On the radio. It seems that the Consties have been working on the case, and they've gotten the murderer's sister to talk.—You're a hell of an investigator!

ELLIS. Who is he?

FRANK. That laboratory worker who'd been to see the Cardinal that afternoon just before Percy Gilman was there. You'll remember he'd once been a Red and then claimed to be converted to Peterism, and had come to talk to the Cardinal about publishing a repudiation of Reddism in one of the Peter papers.

GANDERSHEIM. How did he manage the murder?

FRANK. They haven't gotten him to tell yet, but he'd been working with inflammable gases.

ELLIS. Has he actually confessed to the crime?

FRANK. He doesn't need to: this sister has produced a letter he wrote her that shows he was still a Red long after he was supposed to have been converted. He and she had fallen out, because he'd gone over to Belgrade when she still stuck to the Kremlin—and that's the reason she's decided to expose him.

ELLIS. He may have been a Peter and a Belgradist both. There *are* such people, you know. Since the Peters put up such a struggle in Hungary and Czechoslovakia, the Belgradists have come to terms with them.

FRANK. This fellow was a fanatic, apparently.

ELLIS. But fanatical about what? I saw the thing that he wrote, and it was all against the Kremlin.

FRANK. Well, put his Reddism with the homicidal gases—

ELLIS. —And you haven't necessarily got a case—

FRANK. It looks enough like a case so that we ought to have known about it. I told you to go after their families.

ELLIS. I don't like pumping people's families.

FRANK. Hell—it's a question of public peril!

ELLIS. Well, I'm glad I didn't have anything to do with making that woman talk—

FRANK. She was evidently crazy to talk.

ELLIS. —And I doubt the value of her evidence.

FRANK. That would come better from you if—

ELLIS (*asserting himself and cutting in on Frank*). You say that you disapprove of the methods these groups are using, but one of the worst features of it is the way they work on people systematically to destroy normal human relationships. There's getting to be a premium on treachery—

A knock on the door interrupts him.

FRANK. Yes?

The Gardener opens the door and, holding his old slouch hat, comes a short way into the room.

THE GARDENER (*to Judith, with an Irish brogue*). I'm sorry to disturb you, ma'am, but did you want me to transplant the hydrangeas the first thing tomorrow morning? I've just done trimmin' them back.

JUDITH. Oh, yes! (*to Gandersheim*) I hope you approve of this. You don't mind our moving them, do you?— moving the hydrangeas to the stable?

65

GANDERSHEIM. Well, I do, rather. I think it would be better, as I told you when you first brought the question up, to cultivate the original color. You'd see that they belong where they are.

JUDITH. Couldn't we move them back there for a while and feed them whatever they need till they're blue or whatever they're supposed to be?

GANDERSHEIM. I should miss them—I shouldn't feel comfortable. I know that a hydrangea border is as out-of-date now as a boa, but, after all, the whole place is "period."

JUDITH. I was going to plant a border of tulips. They'd light up all that rather bleak approach to the house.

GANDERSHEIM. I shouldn't like that at all! I'm afraid I really couldn't face tulips. I've seen them at their most brilliant in Holland, and I must say they absolutely repel me—just a regiment of brash little prongs sticking up like pins in some tiresome map. I like my flowers a little less—bouncing.

THE GARDENER. Sure, you've no need to worry about that, sir; the missus has ordered some breeds that are speckled and striped like salamanders. They're as unwholesome as anything you could wish.

JUDITH. They're deliciously morbid—you'll see. The hydrangeas are just sickly and sloppy now. Come down and look things over for once. You've never really faced it.

GANDERSHEIM. I'm afraid I must do these letters.

FRANK. Go on, Gandy—there's no hurry about those. Let's get this gardening crisis settled. It's absolutely wearing me down, and the flowers have been looking lousy —I think they're suffering from a sense of insecurity.

JUDITH (*to Ellis, sarcastically*). That's another favorite phrase from the forties!

Ellis gives her a brief grin, which registers his resentment of Frank.

FRANK. It's been a permanent condition since then!— Now, go on; go and feed your hydrangeas!

Judith moves toward the door, and Gandersheim and the Gardener follow.

JUDITH (*to Gandersheim*). It seems that they spray them now instead of merely putting stuff in the soil.

GANDERSHEIM. I do think he's right, you know: flowers should never be frightened.

They go out. Frank sits down in one of the chairs on the side of the table nearest the audience; Ellis remains standing.

ELLIS. I'm sorry you think I've fallen down—but I told you I wasn't the man for that job.

FRANK. You ought to have seen that woman.

ELLIS. I've never believed that that fellow had anything to do with the murder. I've seen the papers that they found in his room, and he was certainly bitter against the Reds. On the other hand, if he was a Belgradist, why should he have killed the Cardinal?

FRANK. That's what we ought to have found out.

ELLIS. By the way, though, it's true that the flashlight was already there in the room when Gilman had his interview with the Cardinal.

FRANK. Did he say so?

ELLIS (*dropping into a chair and facing Frank, on the same side of the table*). Yes: he saw it. He noticed that it was on. He'd thought of telling the Cardinal, but the conversation, he says, had already become so strained that there was no opportunity to mention it.

FRANK. You didn't tell me about that.

ELLIS. I only just found out about it.

FRANK. Do you mean to say you didn't ask Percy whether he'd noticed a flashlight there?

ELLIS. I wasn't allowed to see him long, and most of the time we were talking about things that he wanted me to do for him. You told me to ask him what he wanted and do whatever I could. I found out about the flashlight from one of the cops.

FRANK. Just now?

ELLIS. Yes.—I admit I've been a failure, and I was just going to tell you that I want to quit.

FRANK. Now don't get excited—I don't want you to quit.

ELLIS. I'm no good to you as a detective.

FRANK. You're new at it, that's all. But don't worry. We can drop our own investigation. I need you here now.

ELLIS. I meant, quit the job entirely.

FRANK. Leave the magazine, you mean?

ELLIS. Yes: you've got Gandersheim, and you don't really need me now.

FRANK. He can't do everything: he's got to write his stories.

68

ELLIS. I understand he has an irresistible magic for exorcising undesirable visitors.

FRANK. To tell you the truth, Ellis, this shop has been getting a little *too* four-dimensional since Gandersheim has been handling things. I like to have everything in black and white, and I miss your clear-cut methods.

ELLIS. You can easily get somebody else who'll copy out the letters in a big round hand.

FRANK. It's the *point of view* I can't get. You have the *Spotlight* point of view.

ELLIS. But what *is* the *Spotlight* point of view? It's having no point of view at all.

FRANK. I thought you were sympathetic with what I'm trying to do.

ELLIS. I am, I suppose—but good Lord, I can't see that you make very much impression on the tendencies you're trying to check.

FRANK. Well, the circulation's going up—we're certainly not doing badly—and I don't exactly see you happy on the ordinary commercial mag just pulling down big pay.

ELLIS. I could make enough money in a couple of years to knock off and do a novel.

FRANK. Have you actually had an offer?

ELLIS. Yes.

FRANK. From a magazine?

ELLIS. Yes.

FRANK. Well, don't kid yourself a minute: it's just like Hollywood used to be—you're not too young to remember that, are you?—or like the advertizing business. You'd find in a couple of years that, instead of having accumulated ideas, you'd been completely emptied of content. (*Getting up and standing over Ellis as he becomes more emphatic and eloquent.*) What the hell will you write about? Expose the magazine racket? That's almost as damaging to self-respect as to keep on cashing in on it. It's a confession that you've been wasting the best years of your life doing something you knew was rotten—and when you come to write (*with an underlining ironic inflection*) your *devastating satire,* you'll find out that your own goddam exposé will sound as cheap as the stuff you're denouncing!

ELLIS. You paint a grim picture—but the kind of thing they want me to write couldn't be very degrading.

FRANK. Who's "they"?

ELLIS (*getting up and picking up his briefcase*). I've been asked not to talk about it.

FRANK. More secrecy! I send you out to try to clear up a mystery, and you come back all swaddled in secrets! Well, go ahead, get in on the big dough!—but don't do it just because you're sore.

Gandersheim comes into the room.

GANDERSHEIM (*to Frank*). If you'll pardon me just a moment, I want to look something up in the gardening encyclopedia. We used to have an old one here.

FRANK. Go ahead—all your books are still there.

Gandersheim goes over to the bookcase at the right of the fireplace.

ELLIS (*to Frank, picking up the briefcase*). I'll just

take care of this stuff I brought out. May I go down to your room, where it's quicker?

FRANK (*morosely*). Go ahead.

GANDERSHEIM (*taking down a volume*). I suppose this is quite out of date. Judith says they spray them now.

FRANK. This is a hell of a note! Ellis has just announced he's quitting.

GANDERSHEIM (*looking up*). Leaving the magazine?

FRANK. He's got an offer from somebody—he won't tell who. But I'm damned if I can see why he should want to go!

GANDERSHEIM. I'm not entirely surprised.

FRANK. What do you mean?

GANDERSHEIM. Well, I hesitate to mention the matter —and anything I say, you understand, is said in the strictest confidence.

FRANK. Go ahead.

GANDERSHEIM. Well, I believe that Ellis—who is a very well-brought-up young man—has a very strong sense of honor.

FRANK. So he was telling me.

GANDERSHEIM. Oh, I don't mean the reporting thing— I don't mean about the sister.

FRANK. What *do* you mean?

GANDERSHEIM. Well, I don't really think that he'd want to stay on with *Spotlight*, if—if—well, if he was in a position in which he felt he was abusing your confidence.

FRANK. You mean he's gone over to the Reds?

71

GANDERSHEIM. No, no: I meant something more personal.

A pause: Frank stands frowning and brooding. Gandersheim finds the place in the book.

FRANK. You don't mean Judith?

GANDERSHEIM (*looking up for a moment, then examining the encyclopedia article*). On his side a little, perhaps.

FRANK. What gives you that idea?

GANDERSHEIM. Well, one notices certain things—and quite without design on my part, I overheard a conversation just now—

Judith comes in.

JUDITH (*to Gandersheim*). You got away from me before I was done with you.

GANDERSHEIM. I just came up here to look up the hydrangeas. It turns out to be rather complicated. I should have to take it up with the gardener.

JUDITH. I wanted you to go all over the place with me, but you slipped away into the pergola and when we looked there, you'd disappeared.

GANDERSHEIM (*flustered by Judith's appearance*). I'm entirely at your service.

JUDITH. Don't be scared: I'm not going to try to put anything more over on you. (*To Frank.*) He did give in about the tulips.

GANDERSHEIM. So very few things nowadays are allowed to remain the same.

FRANK. Go on and thrash it out with the gardener, Gandy—I want to talk to Judith.

JUDITH (*to Frank*). If he succeeds in escaping me now, I'm afraid I'll never get him again!

GANDERSHEIM. I don't see that you really need me, since you've quite made up your mind about everything.

FRANK (*to Judith*). Let him alone—let him talk to the gardener: he'll get along better without you.

Gandersheim, leaving the book on the long table, goes out with a piqued air of dignity. Frank pretends to look at a manuscript till Gandersheim has left the room.

JUDITH (*hardly waiting for the door to close*). I hope you don't think it's a treat for me to have the landlord living here with us and interfering with all my arrangements.

FRANK. He's certainly been a godsend to *me*.

JUDITH. I don't think you ought to let him do so much —especially answering letters. You've already got the reputation of being an eccentric and a crank, and now people will say you're crazy.

FRANK. It at least means that *you* don't have to attend to them. You were complaining that you'd have to do everything. In some ways he's the most satisfactory person that I've ever had on that job.

JUDITH. That's just because he turns cartwheels for you whenever you open your mouth. He's absolutely infatuated with you.

FRANK. I'm glad somebody is.

JUDITH. If I were you, I'd be embarrassed.

FRANK. The only thing I find embarrassing is having you be rude to Gandy—and openly hostile to me.

JUDITH. I'm sorry, Frank, but this whole situation has

73

become absolutely impossible. I was just going to tell you: I want to get a job in town.

FRANK. What's the matter now?

JUDITH. I can't go on like this. I've got nothing to do out here.

FRANK. I thought that you were just telling me that housekeeping was giving you so much to do that you had no time for anything else!

JUDITH. The trouble is I'm not a housewife. I've tried it, and I know I'm no good at it.

FRANK. Yes, you are.

JUDITH. No, I'm not. I don't have any chance at all to do the kind of thing I *can* do.

FRANK. You've been wonderful with the magazine.

JUDITH. You want to be the whole thing yourself— you don't even really want my suggestions.

FRANK. That isn't true at all—on the contrary—

JUDITH. I've decided that the moment for a break has come. I'm losing all my resiliency out here. Jane Maclanihan said to me the other day that I'd become so suburban and wholesome that she could hardly believe I was the same girl who'd made the Dean cry at college.

FRANK. You're better looking now than you ever were! It's the first time you've ever been tanned.

JUDITH. I'm not the type that ought to be tanned. I wanted to try this tennis-playing life, but now that I've had it, it bores me. I can't be a young country club matron—especially when you won't go near the club—and even the club out here is second-rate.

FRANK. Sit down and let's talk about it.

JUDITH. I don't want to sit down and talk about it. We've talked about it enough.

FRANK. What's the matter lately?

JUDITH. Nothing's the matter except that I've made up my mind.

FRANK. Well, you've chosen a fine time to walk out on me. Did you know that Ellis was quitting?

JUDITH. Did you fire him?

FRANK. No, of course I didn't fire him. Somebody's offered him what he thinks is a better job.

JUDITH. I'm not surprised, the way you've been treating him.

FRANK. What do you mean, the way I've been treating him?

JUDITH. You were insulting to him just now.

FRANK. No, I wasn't.

JUDITH. Of course you were. You're such a born bully that you're not even able to realize that you're habitually insulting to people.

FRANK. On the contrary, *you* bully *me*: you've got me afraid to open my mouth.— (*Expostulating and waving his arms.*) Listen, Judy: when you and I work together, we're wonderful—we can stand up to anything. We're united in browbeating the rest of the world, and that's what you have to do nowadays, if you don't want to get flattened out yourself. But when we break loose against one another, we simply use up all our energies and don't accomplish anything.

JUDITH. That's why I think it's so much better for each of us to be independent.

FRANK (*coming over to her and taking both her hands*). Listen, darling: you know that I can't live without you.

JUDITH. Those nostalgic clichés of yours? I wish you could get along without them when you're making your big scenes.

FRANK. Did you ever hear anybody say in a play: "We can't go on like this!"? *I* have, a hell of a lot of times.

JUDITH. Yes, of course: the whole thing is old hat—this is the kind of perfectly obvious situation that there's no point in making a fuss about.

FRANK. Now, look here—(*he puts his arm around her and leads her over to the head of the table*) I want you to sit down a minute and listen to me talk—

JUDITH. I've been doing that for years.

FRANK. Not many.

JUDITH. Four.

FRANK. All right, but this is not a mere oration. Sit down here. (*He makes her sit down in the first chair at the right behind the table and takes his place in the highbacked chair at the head.*)

JUDITH. You're going to tell me that you divorced your wife to marry me, and that I prevent you from seeing your daughter.

FRANK. No, I'm not.

JUDITH. You usually do at this point.

FRANK. First of all, what I want to say is that you ought to know it's actually true when I tell you that I can't get along without you. It's not a cliché, it's the literal fact. You've been the mainspring of *Spotlight*—you inspired it in the first place. Everything I've done

76

since I've known you has been done on account of you. Though I'd been a fair success before, it had only been as a glorified hack. I was an old-style newspaper man, well on the way to obsolescence—and the big turning-point in my life was that night when I lectured at your college and you came up to ask me questions, with your hair done up in a bun and your panther eyes flashing out challenge. Do you remember that you said to me that F. D. R. had the virtues of a tactful hostess?—that he knew how to diminish friction and prevent disagreeable incidents, but had no real ideas of his own? Do you remember how you said that?

JUDITH (*pleased as always at praise but not wanting to acknowledge it*). No.

FRANK. Well, it made a sensational impression on me. I was jolted and shocked at first, but then I was released, delighted. It was just what I'd been thinking myself but wouldn't have had the nerve to say or wouldn't have been able to say that well. I thought that you were the brightest girl I'd ever seen. I hadn't known such girls existed—and I don't believe they ever did before. What's always been miraculous to me and what's given me such guts as I've had lately has been just exactly that fact: that an obstinate old-timer like me, a journalist who still takes journalism seriously, an American who still believes that this country has a great contribution to make to the progress of human civilization—that a person like me had made contact, an actual vital contact, with one of the most gifted young people of your nineteen-forty crop that grew up without any illusions. The thing that I was

77

proudest of was your telling me that you had more respect for me than for the boys of your own generation.
Do you remember telling me that?

JUDITH (*in a tone which implies that she remembers
but is no longer interested in it*). Yes.

FRANK. I don't want to hand myself bouquets, but I
think I did give you something. You kids were born into
a world where the money had all blown up and nobody
knew where they were at. The first batch consoled themselves with Communism, but then, when Soviet Russia
went bad, they didn't know where the hell to turn. The
next batch were shipped off to war, which they weren't
enthusiastic about, and the later ones who'd missed the
war found themselves shunted off into compulsory military training, with the prospect of another war which
they were even less enthusiastic about. Now, *I'd* had the
luck to grow up in a small-sized Western city, where my
dad ran an independent paper and where he'd somehow
managed to survive as a ring-tailed gyascutus of Popu-
lism from the heroic Bryan period—

JUDITH. I've heard all this before, you know.

FRANK. Not so eloquently expressed, have you?—What
I wanted to say was simply that you gave me the spark
that ignited me—that made me flame up again when I
might well have smouldered out—

JUDITH. Oh, Frank, your old moth-eaten metaphors!

FRANK (*going on even more ardently, since he knows
that, in spite of her mockery, she is gratified by his admiration*). "Flame up" is the only way to say it—it isn't
even a metaphor. At that time you were a burning brand,

but you were just being reckless and negative—your audacity had no real object—

JUDITH. My flame has been burning so low lately that it's more like a pilot-light on one of those gas-ranges, and if I don't have a new cylinder put in, there's just going to be a faint bad smell and you'll know that the gas has gone out.

FRANK. And is Ellis your new cylinder?—(*with sarcasm*) to carry on with your up-to-date imagery.

JUDITH. I knew that was coming!

FRANK. Well? (*She does not reply: he gets up.*) You haven't answered my question.

JUDITH. There's nothing between Ellis and me.

FRANK. You were complaining that you missed him so much.

JUDITH. Why shouldn't I? He's closer to me than you are, because he's nearer my age. We can understand one another with just a look—just an inflection—we don't have to have all these long arguments and historical recapitulations.

FRANK. And that's why you want to go to town, isn't it?

JUDITH. Is what why I want to go to town?

FRANK. You've made him throw up his job! I don't think he had any idea of it when I saw him before he came upstairs. You'd talked to him in between.

JUDITH. He didn't say a word to me about his job.

FRANK. You influenced him to throw it up.

JUDITH. You influenced him yourself by being so nasty to him.

79

FRANK. I don't think he was sore at me. The trouble was that you'd gotten him interested in you, and he thought he was being disloyal.

JUDITH (*getting up*). I won't stand for this any more! If there were no other reason for getting away, these continual scenes of jealousy would be enough.

FRANK. So you walk out on me at the worst possible moment! Just because you were deserted yourself, you try to revenge yourself by. walking out on other people!

JUDITH. What do you mean I was deserted?

FRANK. You were deserted by your parents—you lost them before you were six years old. And you've been behaving all your life as if you'd never grown any older.

JUDITH. This psychoanalytic routine of yours is just as old-fashioned now as your sentiments from Victorian novels.

FRANK. You can't help being bitter, maybe—but I think you ought to keep it well in mind what you're really being bitter about. It's not me—it's not anything *I've* done to you—

JUDITH. You promised you wouldn't talk about that.

FRANK (*determined, in desperation, to make some impression on her*). You ought to be reminded of it when you're trying to blame somebody else for the fact that your parents—

JUDITH (*resisting in real alarm*). Now, don't!

FRANK. —For the fact that your parents were victims of the damned frauds and swindles of Wall Street—

JUDITH. You promised. If you break your promise, I'll never have any more respect for you!

FRANK. That your father was ruined in the Crash, and that he shot your mother and then shot himself when you were in the next room. (*She becomes pale and rigid, cannot speak.*) I'm sorry, but I brought it out on purpose —because I think you ought to face it. You're making a big mistake when you try to shut it out of your mind: that only gets you all confused. It makes you think that I'm your father, so that you work up a grudge against me—a completely irrational grudge. *I'm* not your father —I'm your husband. I love you—I love you, darling—and it's a hell of a raw deal for me to have to be identified with him—

JUDITH (*screaming*). Oh, how can you? How can you? You promised me you never would! How can you, you great horrible lout! (*She throws a magazine from the table at him.*) You pretentious small-time tyrant!

FRANK (*coming over to her*). Don't—I'm sorry—

JUDITH (*hysterical, grasping his hands, as he tries to put his arms around her*). Don't hit me!

FRANK. I'm not going to hit you.

JUDITH. You want to kill me! (*Shrieking.*) Help!

Gandersheim opens the door and enters; the Gardener hangs behind in the doorway.

GANDERSHEIM. I'm sorry: did I interrupt something? *Judith leaves the room, weeping.*

FRANK. Judith is a little upset: she sometimes gets into these states.

GANDERSHEIM. I'm sorry. Is there anything I can do?

FRANK. No, thanks. She'll be all right.

81

GANDERSHEIM. I was just bringing the gardener in to show him the encyclopedia.

FRANK. Go ahead.

He hurries out.

GANDERSHEIM (*to the Gardener*). Come in. I'll just read you what it says.

He picks up the volume from the table and finds the place again. The room is already half dark, and he carries the book over to the window-seat. He is agitated but tries to hide it and sits down behind the table to consult the book. During the conversation that follows, the room is growing dark.

GANDERSHEIM. You know, they're rather curious botanically. The things that you think are the flowers are actually sexless and sterile: they don't have either stamens or pistil. But they certainly make a brave showing! —that is, when they're properly nourished—and that's our problem now: to get them back to their brilliant blue. They do look rather livid now—as if the dye were all running out of them. A brilliant and frightening blue— I've always found blue rather frightening—and the color does have its significance in connection with my life in this house. My mother had piercing blue eyes, but it isn't only my mother's eyes. It's got something to do with the blues—I don't mean the musical blues, but what I used to call *le cafard blafard*—that's a French phrase I made up once. I thought I couldn't stand it here at first when she wouldn't send me back to school, but I managed to settle down to it and somehow nourished myself—I exploited the elements that made me blue, just as we

82

hope our hortensias will—that's a much more beautiful name for them, I think—and I got to like the old blue border, because it represented my mood.—(*Looking up from the book.*) Tell me, do you believe in dreams? I see now that you're really an Irishman—and all you Irish are great dreamers, aren't you?

THE GARDENER. Sure, it's the quare dream I had last night: I thought that God had opened up the future and revealed to me some of the surprises that he had up his sleeve for the human race. I was flattered and proud at first to be taken into the Almighty's confidence, but when I woke up this morning, I wished that he'd kept his own counsel and not let me in on his plans.

GANDERSHEIM. Pretty discouraging, eh?

THE GARDENER. Sure, it was appalling entirely. It threw a scare into me I'm not over yet. I don't belong with these craytures, I kept telling myself: they're not men even, they've lost touch with God.

GANDERSHEIM. You felt that you were helpless against them?

THE GARDENER. I felt that I was helpless to save them.

GANDERSHEIM. I've been having the most dreadful dreams—just since I've been back in this house. But in my case, I'm up against a gang—Shidnats Slyme's gang. I created Shidnats Slyme, of course, but somehow it's outside me, beyond my control. I dream I'm walking up to the door of a house in a perfectly normal street. The sun is out and everything is cheerful—the people are all going about their business. I knock; no one answers; I go in. The house is completely empty and perfectly commonplace. But there's a thing waiting for me in there—quietly waiting for me: *I* have to come to *it*. I walk through the rooms and the hallway and out through the backdoor—and there in the backyard, just hanging in the air above my head, is the *paralyzing unspeakable thing*. It makes my blood run cold just to think of it, and I haven't even had the courage to put it into one of my stories! It's just a little spark of blue light that might be made by crossed electric wires—but I know that I can't resist it, that it's certainly going to get me. I always wake up at that point, but even then I can't shake it off. I'm trembling—frightened to death—sunk in the most hideous despair—and I don't know why it should be—I can't make out where the image comes from. It's just a quiet little point of light, but it's pitiless, it's infinitely cruel!

THE GARDENER. Would ye care to say what's frightened ye most in your life?

GANDERSHEIM. Oh, it would be hard to say. I've always been subject to panics of the kind that are called irrational—as if something were going to pounce on me, to take possession of me. I had a touch of it just now outside when she was bullying me about the hydrangeas—and then when we walked in on that scene, I was suddenly all unnerved!

THE GARDENER. Would it maybe be the piercing blue eye that you say your mother had—that little blue light you're scared of?

GANDERSHEIM. Oh, please! I've been through Freud.

THE GARDENER. And did you not learn anything from it?

GANDERSHEIM. I read it like fiction and got bored with the plots—and even more with some of my friends who fancied themselves as Freudian characters.

THE GARDENER. Sure, it's true that the case-histories have turned into myths and that people feel they have to act them out. But there's some truth in all great myths. They can teach us what to expect.

GANDERSHEIM. What a knowledgeable old chap you are! My childhood does come back on me rather here, with everything that was nastiest about it. But I don't know where else to go.

THE GARDENER. I'm in the same situation meself.

GANDERSHEIM. You've never thought of going back to the old country?

THE GARDENER. To Ireland? Faith, Ireland today is as bad as the rest of the world!

GANDERSHEIM. The Irish have at least won their freedom.

THE GARDENER. They've won their freedom the same way as the Russians. They've lost all their men of vision. When they were victims of a monarchical tyranny, they had rebels, and the rebels had the luxury of heroism and oratory, prophecy and literature. But when the people came into their own, they were content to be tyrannized over by police captains and politicians, paperwork-men and priests.

GANDERSHEIM (smiling). You're a clever old boy. You've cheered me up.

THE GARDENER. Don't be scared of the lady, sir.

GANDERSHEIM. My mother?

THE GARDENER. That, too.

GANDERSHEIM. You mean Judith?

THE GARDENER. She's far more scared than you.

GANDERSHEIM. Do you think so?

THE GARDENER. Sure, she's frightened of her own shadow, for she thinks it must cast a contagion on everything it falls upon.

GANDERSHEIM. On account of that dreadful thing, you mean?—her father shooting her mother?

THE GARDENER. It's both grievance and guilt she feels, and nothing can make up the loss.

GANDERSHEIM. One could pity her a little more easily if she weren't so extremely aggressive. I really can't take it from her! When she scored off me just now—when she made me sacrifice those hydrangeas—I couldn't resist my little revenge—though it may have been rather unfair—it did upset me when I heard her screaming. Not that *she* would have hesitated a moment to take advantage of *me*. She's one of these modern women who want to have equality for the sexes, but they *don't* have the same sense of honor as men, and you can't always meekly submit to being made a ninny of. There are moments in modern life when you have to fight a bitch in the same spirit.

THE GARDENER (*interrupting him*). Sure, you can't see to read by that light. (*He turns on one of the student lamps and moves it up to illuminate the book.*) Now what has the encyclopedia to tell us about the hydrangeas?

GANDERSHEIM. Thank you. Oh, yes: let me see. Here it is: you put iron or alum in the soil.— (*Looking up at the Gardener and smiling.*) If we could really revive the hydrangeas, if we could get them to blaze a splendiferous blue, we might be able to make that wicked little light look a bit dimmer and weaker. Do you think so?—I'm just talking nonsense—it's only poetical nonsense. One doesn't have to explain poetry to an Irishman.

THE GARDENER (*reading over his shoulder*). "Late in autumn, after frost, when the leaves have fallen, the plants may be moved to a frost-proof cellar and kept rather dry till spring. They may then be repotted with new soil."

GANDERSHEIM. I do hope they won't die in the meantime!

SCENE 2

The same room. Early December: eleven o'clock in the morning. Frank and Gandersheim are sitting at the table —Frank in the highbacked chair, Gandersheim about four feet away from him, on the opposite side from the audience. Gandersheim has lying before him a neat pile of manuscripts, on the top page of each of which has been clipped a yellow piece of paper for the editors to write their comments on; Frank is sorting out a more disorderly lot. He picks up a typewritten list.

FRANK. Well, here's the contents of the first January issue. First: *A Slap-Happy New Year.* That's an editorial by me. My idea is that the American people have taken such a beating in the last election that such of them as are rejoicing over it are actually goofy with punishment. *(He hands the manuscript to Gandersheim, who laughs appreciatively as he lays it face down beside him.) The*

88

Washington Iron Curtain. "Iron Curtain" is a hell of an old phrase now—and what I'd really like to call it is *The United States: Top Secret*—but I wanted to write a leader called *Is the Human Race Top Secret?*

GANDERSHEIM. That's brilliant. Why don't you save it then?

FRANK. That's what I think I will. All right: let the Iron Curtain go. (*He hands the article to Gandersheim, who does with it as before.*) Maybe we'll think of something better later. The next is *The Mechanical Brain and the Gettysburg Address.*

GANDERSHEIM. I haven't seen that.

FRANK. It's a hell of a good article! (*He hands it to him, and Gandersheim glances at it.*) It shows that this so-called machine that thinks may be able to play chess and translate and correct examination papers, but it couldn't produce a Gettysburg Address—that is to say, if you set it for the occasion and place and for a certain number of words, the best it could possibly do would be string a lot of clichés together.—*Twentieth Floor Express: An Elevator-Man Looks at Life.* You've got that. Did you fix it up?

GANDERSHEIM (*taking it out of his pile and putting it with the others*). I did the best I could.

FRANK. It's interesting, though, don't you think? His impulse to drop the elevator with everybody in it at lunch hour?

GANDERSHEIM (*smiling*). Yes. The only thing I'm dubious about is the title: *An Elevator-Man Looks at Life.*

89

There've been so many people for so many years looking at so many things.

FRANK. Well, my policy is not to worry about what the customers want, but you can't be jolting them *all* the time: they've got to have a few things they're used to. —Next: *Pressure Personalities, Five (handing it to Gandersheim, who looks to see the rest of the title before adding it to the pile as before).* This one is Luke Teniakis. You know, he's that smart young Greek at the head of the big Relief Bureau that gets jobs for refugees and D.P.'s. He's one of the less important figures—but the article last month was hot and the February one will be hotter still, so we can afford to let it smoulder for an issue.—Then here's a nostalgic piece: *When We Skated in Rockerfeller Plaza: A Glimpse of Old New York.* *(Gandersheim finds it.)* OK. Here's the First of a new series: *My Moment of Supreme Indifference. (He finds the manuscript and hands it to Gandersheim.)* That's the name of the series. You know there've been a couple of series like that in other magazines: one on *The Happiest Moment of My Life* and one on *My Proudest Day.* Well, I thought it would be a good idea to have people write up the moments when they felt the most complete indifference about the things that they were supposed to take seriously.

GANDERSHEIM. I didn't know about that either. Was it your idea?

FRANK. No: Judy's.

GANDERSHEIM. Oh!

FRANK. This first one's maybe a bit obvious: *When I Missed the Train for my Wedding.*

GANDERSHEIM (*smiling on one side of his mouth*). That will offend people, won't it?

FRANK. Just scandalize them a little. The others strike more of a heroic note—about people who felt perfect indifference when they thought they were falling to their deaths in planes or missing out on their Hollywood options.—Then here's the second political: *Did the Election Lose Us Our Liberties?*—And special American problems: *Can the Apache Be Saved from Extinction?* (*He looks for the manuscript.*)

GANDERSHEIM. Do you want those two question-titles?

FRANK. Right you are. (*He rewrites one of them.*) *The Twilight of the Apache.* All right. (*He hands Gandersheim the articles.*) —*When the Rue de la Paix Moved to Seventh Avenue.* That's the only article for women this month—but it'll have to be enough. (*He looks for the manuscript.*)

GANDERSHEIM. I don't think we ought to cater to them. That's the trouble with American magazines. They're all just as feminine as *Harper's Brazeer.*

FRANK. That's always been my idea. Goddam it, the very sports departments are written for women now. *You've* got that one, haven't you? (*Gandersheim looks in his pile.*)—Next number: *Pretzel-Bending: A Vanishing Skill.* You've got that one, too.

GANDERSHEIM (*taking them out*). You don't think we're overdoing the nostalgic note just a tiny bit this month?

FRANK. How do you mean?

GANDERSHEIM. Well, it seems to me we're saying farewell to such a lot of things: we're kissing the Apaches good-by—and pretzels and our political liberties and skating in Rockerfeller Plaza, all in the same issue.

FRANK (*studying the list*). By God, I believe you're right.

GANDERSHEIM. I suggest taking out the pretzels and putting in *The Slot-Machine Swindle*—we've had it around for a year.

FRANK. I can't seem to bring myself to run that damn thing. When I reread it, I have the feeling that it's just on the borderline of being ridiculous. The slot-machine isn't always working, so the customer loses his nickel or doesn't get his gum—so what? It makes our exposés look so picayune. But all right: put it in. Let's get it over with!—Now we come (*with his ironical emphasis*) to your *monsterpiece,* which hasn't materialized yet: *The Horror at the North Window: The Professor Faces Shidnats.*

GANDERSHEIM. I'll have it ready by the end of the week. I'm finding it more difficult than usual. I want to have Shidnats Slyme appear, and he's never been described directly—

FRANK. He'd better be sensationally horrible after the build-up you've been giving him for years.

GANDERSHEIM. It will take a little doing. I'm not really sure how he looks—whether he's frightening in an obvious way or something that seems innocent in itself—something like a little blue light.

FRANK. I thought he was a hideous monster.

GANDERSHEIM. The other thing has great possibilities —a terrible little blue light—

FRANK. That's too abstract: your readers would feel they weren't getting their money's worth.

GANDERSHEIM. That's why I must get it exactly right.

FRANK. Better stick to your original idea and make it some kind of hair-raising demon.

GANDERSHEIM. That's just why the other would be more of a surprise. The Professor is looking out the window, and he sees something that he takes at first for a star that he doesn't recognize—but then he becomes aware that it's hanging right over the garden—then it seems to be closer to the window, half a dozen feet beyond the pane. (*He turns toward the bay-window and gestures; Frank looks toward the window, too.*) The next time, it's there in the room—even though the electric lights are on: doesn't that give you a queer twinge?—quietly and steadily shining, but with devilish deadly intensity—with a ray like an old-fashioned hatpin that will pierce right through to your brain—

FRANK. Well, that's an unpleasant thought, but it seems to me a little too special. All I can say is that, as a Gandersheim fan, I'll be bitterly disappointed if I don't get a bang-up bugaboo with a definite personality.

GANDERSHEIM. I'm not sure that Shidnats has anything so human as what we'd call a personality. He takes possession of other people's personalities. In his non-incarnate state, he's simply a force that blights and kills, the cruellest thing that exists—

FRANK. You wouldn't gather that from the name? —Where did you get that name, by the way?

GANDERSHEIM (*smiling slyly*). It's never been explained in the stories, but a few of my readers have guessed. Do you know what my initials stand for?—the initials of my real name?

FRANK. M. S.? No: what?

GANDERSHEIM. Myles Standish. (*He pauses expectantly.*)

FRANK. I don't get it.

GANDERSHEIM. Spell Myles Standish backwards.

FRANK (*grinning*). I see! But why treat a good name like that?

GANDERSHEIM. It's a real desecration, I know. I was named after Myles Standish, because he was an ancestor of mine. But it was something I cooked up as a boy. Actually, I was awfully proud of coming of *Mayflower* stock. All the people around here were much richer than we— they were all manufacturers and suchlike. My father was a business man, too, but I liked to think that we were different, because he was a linen importer, and the firm was very old, with a distinguished brass plate on the building. But what I was proudest of was my connection with Myles Standish. I thought I had the right to despise all those people who made baking-powder and hardware, because they were parvenus—however much they might be rolling in money and however much they might beat me at tennis.

FRANK. Then why pervert your *Mayflower* name?

GANDERSHEIM. My fantasy was that I was Myles Standish—that Myles Standish was among them and they didn't know it, weren't able to appreciate him. They thought I was just a sissy, a hateful little brat, but all the time I was one of the giants, the leader of the Plymouth Colony, an instrument chosen by a jealous God to make His will prevail. And yet, while Big Business prevailed, I had to work underground, I had to assume a disguise— so I turned my name around to make it sound as outlandish and unsavory as I thought they must think I was—

FRANK. That would be a story in itself—you ought to write it someday—but in the meantime, won't you kindly get to work on *The Horror at the North Window?* Thursday's your deadline, remember. (*He goes on reading his list.*) Well, here's the sporting piece: *Muskallonge-Fishing in Michigan.* (*Finding it and picking it up.*) We've got to get a better title.

GANDERSHEIM. *Unmasking the Muskallonge?*

FRANK. I don't see the point to that.

GANDERSHEIM. Well, it says that—   .

FRANK. *Misleading the Muskallonge*—that's no good either. *Outsmarting the Muskallonge!*—that'll do. (*He changes the title with his pencil.*) *Outsmarting the Muskallonge.*—And finally, Judy's nightlife—it hasn't been seen, I suppose?

GANDERSHEIM. Not yet.

FRANK. Jesus, I wish she'd at least call me up! She wanted to catch the opening of Pinky's Place, but that was two nights ago. It's a hell of a damn nuisance having your wife as a regular contributor!

95

GANDERSHEIM. What a hit her articles are making, though!

FRANK. I hope they're worth the price I pay for them! She's away now practically the whole week. The household is going to pieces, and if I want to see anything of her, I have to go up to town and spend an evening in some gruesome dive.

GANDERSHEIM. She and Ellis, I understand, are often seen together.

FRANK (*disregarding this*). I don't see what people get out of those places! Have you been to a nightclub lately? They're mass propositions now, just like everything else. They remind you of the old-fashioned beer-gardens, except that they don't have any of the things that used to make beer-gardens comfortable. They're so crowded and noisy that you can't talk, and they're so airless that they give you a headache. And before every act in the show, there's a goddam propaganda spiel, in which somebody explains that the trained seals are products of Red education and that the hillbilly folk-songs have got something to do with the Americanism of the snob Elitists.

GANDERSHEIM. Judy seems to find them worth while.

FRANK. The kids of her age never knew a time when anything was any good.

GANDERSHEIM. No: of course, they've never known—but *we* know.—We have many things in common, Frank. I feel sometimes that you and I are different aspects of the same person!

FRANK (*not much liking this*). I don't see that entirely.

GANDERSHEIM (*slightly hurt*). Oh, I don't mean we

aren't very different in a great many obvious ways. Of course, I'm an Easterner, an aesthete, what's usually called a dreamer— (*Frank picks up a pile of mail and begins going through it rapidly, tearing the envelopes open, glancing at the enclosures and throwing them aside.*) I've travelled, become cosmopolitan; while you're very much the Westerner and the rugged practical man: you stick by the country and its *mores*. And yet both of us represent the same old American thing: an individualistic idealism. We're two faces of the same coin—and it was written that we should land up here, in this funny old house of mine, working on the same brave project. Deep down, we're inseparable, inextricable. Nobody who hadn't been bred in the American tradition of *The Rights of Man* could have launched a magazine like *Spotlight;* and I think I can say that no one who didn't have Melville and Poe in his blood could ever have—

FRANK (*staring at a letter he has opened*). Well, I'm a son of a bitch!

GANDERSHEIM. What is it?

FRANK. A threat, by God! An anonymous letter!

GANDERSHEIM. Let me see it. (*He takes the letter.*) How curious! It's not illiterate, as so many anonymous letters are.

FRANK (*getting up and standing behind him*). Look at the way it reads! It's as pompous as an official communication! (*reading*) "Frank Brock is hereby notified that, as from date of reception of this letter, he must discontinue at once the publication of his scheduled series, *Pressure Portraits*. The consequence of failing to comply with this order will be prompt incapacitation through violence, in the fullest and most definitive physical meaning of the phrase. This warning is not the production of an unbalanced individual but of a responsible organization devoted to the public interest and provided with improved equipment for the implementation of its policies."

GANDERSHEIM. "Incapacitation through violence in the fullest sense of the phrase"—do you think that means they're threatening to kill you? What a peculiar way to put it!

FRANK. It's simply damn badly written, in this typical bureaucratic jargon that's been rampant ever since the war. If I knew their goddam address, I'd put it into decent English and send it back.

GANDERSHEIM (*still looking at the letter*). You'd better think right away about getting police protection. I wonder what they're threatening to do. You know, I'm convinced that there's some new kind of weapon that nobody's got on to yet. We still don't know how Cardinal Keenan was murdered—and then there was that postmaster in New Rochelle who was found burned to death the other day—the papers didn't pay much attention to it, but it was queer and hasn't been explained.

FRANK. There's no question in my mind that Keenan was put out of the way by the Reds.

GANDERSHEIM. They've never proved it on that fellow, though.

FRANK. We've already had one Red portrait and have just announced another one.

98

GANDERSHEIM. But we've covered all the other groups, too.

FRANK. I suppose I'll have to have a bodyguard. That's a nuisance I'd hoped to avoid—and to hell with it!—I'm not going to do a thing. I'll just go on running the series as scheduled.

GANDERSHEIM. You've got more nerve, Frank, than anybody I've ever known, and I'm right by your side all the time. If they should get you—

FRANK. Is that Judy? (*He listens intently for her step.*)

GANDERSHEIM (*finishing a little lamely*).—They'd get me, too.

Judith enters. She is very smartly dressed; has changed her way of doing her hair and has evidently been given the works at a beauty parlor. She has entirely dropped the magazine editor and is blooming in a new role: that of fascinating woman-about-town. Throughout the scene that follows, she puts on a great show of knowingness, self-assurance and conscious attractiveness, patronizing Frank in a way that would quickly exasperate him if it were not for the seriousness of the situation and the importance of what she has to tell him. He comes over to the door to meet her. Gandersheim nods to her curtly and pretends to busy himself at the other end of the room, then reclines on the window-seat, with his back against the wall opposite the audience, examining manuscripts.

FRANK. I hope you've got your copy with you!

JUDITH. I haven't quite finished it yet. I was going to type it out now.

FRANK. You better get to work right away. It ought to go out by the one o'clock messenger. But before you do anything else, please find out what's wrong in the kitchen. We got a rotten breakfast this morning and I'm not sure we're going to get any lunch.

JUDITH. I've seen Bertha. She says you've been barking at her.

FRANK. Of course I've been barking at her. She brought me coffee that was stone cold.

JUDITH. She says that you made a long telephone call after it was brought in.

FRANK. It was cold when it first arrived. She was definitely opposed to the whole idea of giving us breakfast at all.

JUDITH. You can't expect her to revel in it if you're so disagreeable to her.

FRANK. If you were here, that wouldn't happen—and if you're going to stay away, you might at least get your copy in on time!

JUDITH. I wanted to wait for the opening of the Only Yesterday Club—and it turned out to be the only one that was interesting. They sang old surrealist songs from the Lean Thirties that I could sometimes just remember from my childhood. It's incredible how they liked to talk gibberish then—it was evidently an outlet for them. They had some of the most lunatic popular songs! See if you can make sense of this one:

> "Oh, Mairzy Doats and Dozy Doats
> And little Lamzy Divy"—

FRANK (interrupting). I've just received an interesting

specimen of a different variety of gibberish. Read that. (*He hands her the letter and watches her while she reads it, not without a certain satisfaction as he expects her to be upset.*)

JUDITH (*handing it back to him*). Yes. I'm not surprised. If I were you, I'd stop the series.

FRANK. You'd have me just lay down and take it?

JUDITH. If my guess is right about what this is. The next article's Luke Teniakis, isn't it?

FRANK. One of the least offensive.

JUDITH. That's where you're wrong. Teniakis is the biggest shot of all.

FRANK. That Greek delicatessen-dealer isn't a big shot!

JUDITH. Yes, he is. You just don't know about it.

FRANK. What do you mean?

JUDITH. Well, it has to be gone into at length. (*She sits down on the farther side of the table toward the left, and lights a cigarette.*) But you certainly ought to know.

FRANK. Go on. (*He sits down opposite her, toward the right.*)

JUDITH. Well, I suppose you've got it in your article about how he fought in the Liberation movement that was trying to give Greece a new deal and that was put down by the British with U. S. tanks.

FRANK. Yes.

JUDITH. Well, when the U. S. took over and carried on the British campaign against the revolutionary forces in Greece, Teniakis lost faith in the Allied pretensions, but at the same time he was too independent to want to work for the Reds. At first he tried to build up a movement—

the Federation of Permanent Resistance—with the non-Red Left elements in the other countries, but he soon got discouraged with that: they were just mouldy old socialists and liberals—if you'll excuse my speaking disparagingly of liberals. In the meantime, he'd come over here and had set up his Mediterranean Relief Bureau to feed and find jobs for political refugees and politically-minded D.P.'s—but he soon learned American political methods—the kind that don't have anything to do with philosophies or general principles—and he rapidly built up a machine that controlled an immense number of jobs in all kinds of businesses and institutions—

FRANK. I know all that, too.

JUDITH. What you evidently *don't* know, though, is that the Teniakis organization is now the biggest thing in the country. All the other movements are past their prime, they've been getting corrupt and porous, and Teniakis has been able to permeate them—

FRANK (*resentful at being told all this by Judith*). Permeate them with what?

JUDITH. Why, just with Teniakisites. He began by making little deals with the various political and religious groups in order to get his people placed; but with his brain for intrigue—in his way he's brilliant—he gradually brought pressure to bear on them to give his own men more and more power. It was Luke Teniakis who arranged the truce between the anti-Constitutionalist groups and made it possible for them to win the election, and to all intents and purposes it's Teniakis who's now in the White House. He's got his key men in the Cabinet and in every department of the Government.

FRANK. And why has nobody had any inkling of this?

JUDITH. *You* haven't had any inkling of it, because you hide yourself away out here and don't have any idea of what's going on. I began hearing about it before I'd been in New York a week. But there hasn't been anything in the papers, because Teniakis doesn't want publicity. He wants to be known as just the head of a relief bureau. That's why he's trying to stop your article.

GANDERSHEIM (*sitting up*). Was it Teniakis who killed the Cardinal?

JUDITH. It looks that way. It seems that Cardinal Keenan had put up a very tough fight against the Teniakis machine. He'd threatened to make a public statement.

FRANK. I must admit that that's a damn smart idea to have a movement with no publicity!

JUDITH. The age of propaganda is finished. The old groups have been making more noise just because they're losing their grip. They know that they've got nothing more to offer.

FRANK. But what's the idea behind this movement?

JUDITH. There isn't any idea. You liberals always imagine that there has to be an idea behind things. What was the idea behind Genghis Khan or Alexander the Great? The old groups haven't got any real ideas. The Reds haven't believed in their Communism since sometime in the early thirties. The so-called faith of the Children of Peter is something that no decently educated person—

103

with the exception of a few panicky poets—has been able to take seriously since the seventeenth century. And as for the Yankee Elitists, with all their talk about the Founding Fathers—they'd be denouncing even John Adams, if he should turn up in public life today, as a dangerous demagogue.

FRANK. I haven't heard you hold forth so eloquently since your big valedictory oration.

JUDITH. Well, your irony is out of place. I'm simply trying to tell you the score. It may be rather hard for you to grasp it, but you know you've always said yourself that all any of them wanted was power, and what Luke Teniakis has been doing is simply concentrating on power without bothering about ideas or policies. He says that he had enough of ideologies when he saw how the Greek politicians sat around in cafés talking while the fighters were put in jail. But he believes in free speech—

FRANK. So long as nobody mentions *him*.

JUDITH. Yes: the British left the press free in Greece, and he saw that if people were at liberty to discuss their problems in print, they were less likely to make real trouble. He says that—

FRANK. You've met him?

JUDITH. Just once.

FRANK. What kind of a guy is he?

JUDITH. He's a quiet little man—well-dressed. You wouldn't be likely to notice him unless you were face to face with him, but then everything he does is so definite—

FRANK. He made an impression on you?

JUDITH. Yes—in a way, yes. He's so perfectly matter-of-fact. The point is that he gives people permanent jobs—which is, after all, what they most want. They've been over-drugged with lurid lies.

FRANK. No inspirational hokum, eh?

JUDITH. All they seem to have is their slogan—that's been passed around by word of mouth, but that's supposed to have never been printed: *Rule by the Uncommon Man in the Interest of the Common Man.* From the moment that anybody whatever—no matter how mediocre his abilities are—holds one of Teniakis' jobs, he has the status of Uncommon Man and is entitled to regard other people as common men. They say, though, that as a matter of fact there's a pretty high level of ability among the Teniakis appointees.

FRANK. That has a familiar sound.

JUDITH. It's different from fascism, though. It has no social or political program—and it isn't patriotic.

FRANK. You can't tell me he does it all without any kind of personal cult!

JUDITH. Well, they sometimes call him the greatest Greek since Pericles—but he doesn't encourage that.

FRANK. And you think I ought to knuckle under to the greatest Greek since John Maragon without even putting up a fight?

JUDITH. I don't see what else you can do.

FRANK. Hell, I can't refuse a challenge like that! If what you're telling me's true, it's the greatest story of all time. Not to break it would be journalistic suicide.

JUDITH. If you try to break it now, it'll be actual suicide.

FRANK. Why should they go to such lengths?

JUDITH. Right now is the critical time. If the rank and file of the Peters and the Reds and all the rest of the ideological groups were to find out that their top leaders didn't take the groups' doctrines seriously but were just trafficking in fat jobs, there might be a violent reaction.

FRANK. All the more reason to set off the dynamite!

JUDITH. It would mean putting an end to my articles, but of course you don't care about that! There's nowhere else I could write the way I do in *Spotlight,* but you never consider me!

FRANK. Well, I'm not going to suspend publication, and I don't want to get murdered. But there's a high wall around this place, and there's no reason I can't barricade myself. I'll take it up at once with the Chief of Police.

JUDITH. He may be one of Teniakis' men.

FRANK. Out here?

JUDITH. Why not? He has them everywhere.

FRANK. I can always get people I trust.

JUDITH. You've made Bertha so sore at you now that I wouldn't trust *her* not to betray you.

FRANK. She's all right: I'll charm her again.

JUDITH. Your charm! Do you think you can depend on it?

FRANK. Yes. And then, that old gardener—

Gandersheim, who has been staring out the window,

106

now jumps suddenly from the window-seat and speaks in great excitement.

GANDERSHEIM. The gardener!—here he comes now. Listen, Frank: I see the whole thing! I've really been expecting all this—I've had the sense of it ever since I came here. Teniakis is the *Monster God,* and he's been lurking here all the time. He's here with us in the shape of the gardener! He's coming to us from over there! (*Pointing at the window.*) *Look! the landscape has changed!*

FRANK (*going over to the window*). What do you mean it's changed?

GANDERSHEIM. Those horrible little houses!—that's where he's got his own people. They'll creep in on us from there—they'll close in on us!

FRANK. That's just a real estate development—it's been there all along.

GANDERSHEIM. I'm sure *I've* never seen it before.

JUDITH (*who has come to the window, too*). You didn't see it on account of the trees. It's just that the leaves have fallen.

GANDERSHEIM. But look at that old man!—do you see him? He's coming across the fields from there, and there's something *unheimlich* about him. Haven't you noticed how queer he is?

JUDITH. I do think he's a little bit queer, but he's not really one of your goblins.

GANDERSHEIM. One can't tell who or what he is—even his nationality. I thought he was an Italian at first, and he certainly talked Italian—but then, when I talked to him later, he seemed to have an Irish brogue.

FRANK. I noticed that, too.

GANDERSHEIM. He spoke to me here one day in the strangest, most impudent way, and somehow he got me to talk to him about all kinds of personal things.

JUDITH. He's been impudent to me, too.

GANDERSHEIM. It's Shidnats—Shidnats is real! When I spoke about the little blue spark, he simply turned on the light. He meant that he controlled the switch!

FRANK. He might be a Teniakis agent. (*To Gandersheim.*) Go down and get him in, Gandy. He's on his way to the stable.

GANDERSHEIM. There's something wrong with the stable: all those pigeons dying!

FRANK. Take it easy: you ought to be writing that story instead of acting it out.

GANDERSHEIM. You think I'm crazy, I know, but I definitely feel he's not human. I wouldn't venture into the stable with him.

FRANK. Just ask Bertha to ring for him and tell him I want to see him up here.

GANDERSHEIM. All right, Frank: I may be silly, but you ought to be careful what you say to him!

He goes out, controlling his agitation.

JUDITH (*when Gandersheim has left*). I don't see how you can have him around.

FRANK. I couldn't do without him now.

JUDITH. Don't you think it's rather alarming to have him fly off the handle like that?

FRANK. He's nervous and highstrung—and he's been thinking about his next story.—Tell me: who put you in touch with the Teniakis organization? How did you get your information?

JUDITH. I got it from several sources.

FRANK. If you've met Teniakis himself, you must know some of his agents.

JUDITH. Pinky who runs Pinky's Place—Pinky Papadopoulos—is one of his principal henchmen.

FRANK. You must have known him pretty well for him to tell you all that.

JUDITH. I do know him pretty well.

FRANK. I knew that those nightlife articles were just a pretext to go on the loose!

JUDITH. It seems to me I've done pretty well for you. You told me to pick up what I could—

FRANK. I didn't mean men.

JUDITH. Don't be vulgar—as they used to say in the *fin de siècle* comedies.

FRANK. You've been seeing Ellis, too, I understand.

JUDITH. I went to a nightclub with him. You wouldn't come out that night.

FRANK. Oh, hell, what's the use of all this, with my back against the wall!

JUDITH. That's what I think.

FRANK. If I were bumped off tomorrow, I suppose you'd carry on with the magazine and turn it into an amusement bulletin—and you might make a success of it at that!

Gandersheim returns and goes over to the fireplace, desiring to remain in the background and to keep away from the window.

JUDITH. I couldn't run a magazine!

FRANK. How in the name of Sarony did they take that picture of you?

JUDITH. The one in the plumed hat?

FRANK. No: the one in *Art and Fashion,* with your hair all whirling around you.

JUDITH. They have you lie down on the floor with an electric fan blowing.

FRANK. Well, I'm damned. Quite a change from the Spartan old bun!

JUDITH. They've been photographing that way for ages.

FRANK. The effect is absolutely indecent.

JUDITH. You haven't seen the one with the plumes?

FRANK. No.

JUDITH. You're not going to like that either.

The Gardener appears in the doorway—this time without his hat—looking sober and dignified.

FRANK. Come on in. Sit down.

The Gardener advances in front of the table and, as Frank resumes the highbacked chair, he turns a chair around to face him and sits down near the other end. Judith takes a seat behind the table, between the Gardener and Frank, leaving a chair between Frank and herself. Gandersheim remains in the background.

FRANK. Well, how are you getting along with the work.

THE GARDENER (*with a Scotch accent*). Weel enough.

FRANK. We're going to need another man, though. It's too much of a proposition for you alone—

THE GARDENER. Ah'm no owerwirket: Ah dinna complain.

FRANK. You ought to have somebody to help you, and I've got to have somebody to drive the car, now that Mrs. Brock is so much in town. I thought you might have a friend who could qualify.

THE GARDENER. Ah've no monny acquentances aboot here.

FRANK. How did *you* happen to come to us, by the way? Was it through an employment agency?

THE GARDENER. Ah've never subjected mysel' to the indeegnity o' the auction block.

FRANK. You simply turned up here, huh? How did you know we needed a gardener?

THE GARDENER. Ah'd heard that ye'd moved in here, and Ah cam' on the offchance. Ah'm condemned to such places noo.

JUDITH (*sharply*). What kind of places do you mean?

THE GARDENER. Lonesome places wi' folk like you.

GANDERSHEIM. But why are you condemned to such places?

THE GARDENER. Ah canna leeve in the great cities noo —and it seems that Ah've still monny mair years to sairve.

GANDERSHEIM. How old are you, may one ask?

THE GARDENER. How auld would ye think?

GANDERSHEIM. Why—I'd say in your late sixties.

THE GARDENER. You'd be a long way short o' the mark.

FRANK. This is getting away from the subject. (*To the*

111

Gardener.) Do you happen to know anything about the Teniakis Relief Bureau?

THE GARDENER. Not from pairsonal experience. Ah've heard of it.

FRANK. You're a naturalized citizen, I take it.

THE GARDENER. Ay.

FRANK. What *is* your nationality?

THE GARDENER. Technically speaking, Ah'm just an American—if that's a nationality.

GANDERSHEIM (*coming over to Frank and speaking in a low voice*). He's got a Scotch accent now. (*He sits down in the chair between Judith and Frank.*)

FRANK. Sometimes you sound like an Italian—sometimes you sound like an Irishman—right now you've got a burr like a Scotchman.

THE GARDENER. Ah'd leeved for conseederable peeriods in a variety o' deefferent countries before Ah cam' to the United States, and noo that Ah'm auld, Ah meex them up.

FRANK. Where were you born?—in Europe?

THE GARDENER. Eh, mon, Ah hardly ken. 'Twas somewhere near the Mediterranean, but Ah canna te' ye where. Mah faither was an eeteenirant cobbler, an' mah parents were always on the move.

FRANK. You've heard about the Teniakis Bureau. Would it be a good place, do you think, for me to get a reliable man?

THE GARDENER. Ah'm sairtain that anyone they sent ye wouldna be verra reliable for *you.*

FRANK. Why not?

THE GARDENER. Wi' your eendependent magazine and your ambeetion to stick by your preenciples, they'll do ye whatever meeschief they're able.

FRANK. What do you mean?

THE GARDENER. Eh, ye maun ken what Ah mean, seence ye've ca'ed me in here to question me.

FRANK. How do you come to know so much about it?

THE GARDENER. Ah've a special knack o' kennin' such matters.

FRANK. That's what I thought.—Listen here: you might just as well tell me right now—because otherwise I'll find out for myself: What kind of an agent are you?

THE GARDENER. Ah'm not an agent in your sense o' the worrd. If Ah'm an agent, Ah'm God's agent.

GANDERSHEIM (struck with panic). What God are you the agent of?

THE GARDENER. Not your God, Meester Gandersheim —for he's nothing more nor less than the auld Presbyterian Devil. In this country, ye began with the Puritan God—the hateful auld jealous Jehovah that folk had read about in the Bible. Ah believed in him once mysel', but later Ah cam' to tak' account that ye need not make God a tyrant to maintain a streect regard for your duties. An' when God is a hanging judge, wi' the Devil to ply the gallows, there's like to be hardly a pin to choose between the judge and his hangman. Tak' my word for it: the fear of a cruel God will mak' ye as cruel as the God ye fear.

GANDERSHEIM. Please mind your own business!

THE GARDENER. Dinna fash yersel'—

113

FRANK (*to the Gardener*). Never mind: I didn't get you in here to preach to us. I just wanted to ask your advice about hiring another man.

THE GARDENER. Ah'll help you, sir, in any way Ah can. Ye can count on my loyalty at a' times, if that's what ye want to make sure of.

FRANK. I can, eh? (*He looks at him searchingly, impressed by his tone of sincerity.*)

THE GARDENER. Ay, why should ye not? Ah'm on the same side o' the struggle as you.

FRANK. What struggle?

THE GARDENER. Ay, what, indeed! It's no verra easy to say. We can hardly talk noo aboot Recht an' Wrong, for it's that that's made our hanging judges, an' put the whole world at their maircy, till there's been nothing but hanging judges wi' no releegion behind them.

FRANK. What the hell? haven't we got to believe that the things we want to do are right? I hope you think that this tough Greek is wrong!

THE GARDENER. Ay, but the most we can say for ourselves is that we're conscious o' representing forces that Teniakis doesna ken, and that we hope he's meescalculated and that what *we* represent will prevail.

FRANK. What forces do you mean exactly?

THE GARDENER. Why, the forces alive in this house. The godlike imagination that recreates life through art—Meester Gandersheim has his share of it, though the quality is puir today—and the weell to comprehend and to speak the truth—deteriorated though *that* is—that ye've tried to poot across in *Spotlight.*

114

JUDITH. I suppose I don't contribute anything!

THE GARDENER. You've something to contreebute, if ye will. You've the spirit of a fighter, if ye'd fight for a cause, instead of just wi eendividuals. 'Twas women like you that won the vote and that took your sex out of the keetchen to use their brains for themselves—but today you'll neither carry children nor carry the banner of freedom.

JUDITH. I *am* free.

THE GARDENER. Free for how long and for what?—Wi' the rest o' the wairld enslaved?

JUDITH (*to Frank*). You see what a sententious old bore he is?

FRANK. After all, we more or less asked for it. (*To the Gardener.*) All right: thank you.

THE GARDENER. Dinna distrust me—dinna be feared to call on me. Ye might care to know Ah've never yet died —so presumably Ah canna be keelled.

He goes out. They watch him to the door.

GANDERSHEIM (*still rather nervous*). What did he mean by that?

JUDITH. He's obviously cracked.

FRANK. I don't know.

JUDITH. He's most obnoxious, in any case.

FRANK. He may be some kind of religious fanatic, but I don't see that he's necessarily crazier than anybody else out here. Gandy has got us surrounded with the demons of Shidnats Slyme! You come and tell me I'm caught in the toils of a super-dictatorship that's super-secret and super-sly, so that it's hopeless even to struggle—and how do I know that *that* isn't a product of *your* imagination?

JUDITH. Thank you for your opinion of my judgment! You see that your friend the gardener knows about Teniakis. In the meantime, you're confronted with that letter.

FRANK. I'm going to give it to the police right away.

JUDITH. If I were you, I'd hold out that article.

FRANK. I hate like hell to yield to threats! There's something in what the old man says: we've got to hope we're stronger than they are.

JUDITH. But in this case we're definitely not—and you're putting me in danger, too. They might kidnap me and hold me as a hostage.

FRANK. Yes: you better stay down here.

JUDITH. And both of us get killed together?

FRANK. Well, I can't just weakly submit. You've never wanted me to in the past.

JUDITH. It's never been a case of life or death.

FRANK. Or of your brilliant journalistic activities.

JUDITH. It's so characteristic of you that you should try to make it a question of my vanity when I'm actually in serious danger!

FRANK. Well! — (*He picks out the article from the pile and throws it on the table.*) I won't send it down by this messenger. I'll hold it out for the present and take the matter under consideration. (*He picks up the manuscripts.*) But don't tell me later on that I haven't got any guts.

She makes no reply. He hurries out.

GANDERSHEIM (*to Judith, with bitterness*). You want to destroy his manhood!

116

JUDITH. That's something you'd sympathize with, isn't it? (*She lights a cigarette.*)

GANDERSHEIM. I certainly sympathize with Frank for everything you've been trying to do to him—to humiliate him and break down his confidence.

JUDITH. Do you want him to be actually killed?

GANDERSHEIM (*agitatedly getting together his manuscripts*). I've got my own suspicions about all this!

JUDITH. What do you mean by that?

GANDERSHEIM. I wonder how you ever came to know so much—and you're a friend of Teniakis, it seems.

JUDITH. I suppose you think you're going to tell Frank that I'm in on the conspiracy to shut him up. If you do, I'll tell Frank a few things about you that I heard at the Punchinello Club.

GANDERSHEIM (*getting up from the table, with his papers*). Frank is a very broadminded and understanding person!

JUDITH. His broadmindedness has limitations.

GANDERSHEIM (*escaping from the room*). Well, we'll see who wins out!

She looks after him with a malevolent smile.

Act Three

ACT III

The workroom in the late afternoon of the day before Christmas. On the window-seat is a "gift-wrapped" Christmas package. On the table, a tray with a bottle of Scotch, a bowl of cracked ice, highball glasses and a bottle of soda-water. Frank is sitting in the highbacked chair, reading something that looks like a leaflet. The day has been dark and is growing darker, and he has turned on one of the student-lamps. He looks up quickly and apprehensively, as he hears a step on the stairs, then stands up, drops the leaflet on the table and covers it with some other papers and, putting his right hand in the pocket of his coat, points a revolver through the pocket toward the door, at which he gazes impassively but intently.

Judith comes in. She is now cultivating a different style, that of intriguing femme fatale: *pale and handsome, hair done up on the top of her head, eyebrows*

completely plucked and false ones drawn on as super-
cilious arches, a close-fitting dark suit. She carries in her
left hand, her arm dropped down at her side, a Christ-
mas wreath tied with a large red ribbon.

FRANK. Hello.

JUDITH. Hello.

FRANK. I didn't expect you.

JUDITH. I said I was coming for Christmas.

FRANK. It's a week since I've heard anything from you.

JUDITH. I've been busy. I didn't know just when I
could come.

FRANK. I haven't done anything about Christmas
dinner.

JUDITH. I thought you were going to ask the What's-
Their-Names and the other people for tomorrow afternoon.

She goes over to the mantelpiece and sets the wreath
up in front of the clock.

FRANK. I hadn't heard anything from you.

JUDITH. I told you I was coming.

FRANK (*watching her with the wreath*). That's cock-
eyed. Get the ribbon on the bottom.

JUDITH. Why not at the top?

FRANK. Well, get it in the middle, anyway! (*She ar-*
ranges it with the bow at the bottom.) That still isn't
straight.

JUDITH (*turning around and coming over to get a*
cigarette from the table). You can't make it stand straight
if you have the bow underneath.

FRANK. The What's-Their-Names have asked us to their house for dinner tomorrow night.

JUDITH. I have to go back tomorrow night. I'm going to dinner in town.

FRANK. I told them I didn't know whether you'd be here. Why, as a matter of fact, did you think it was worth while to come?

JUDITH. It wasn't if you're going to behave like this.

FRANK. This is a hell of a merry Christmas! If I'd known you weren't going to take it seriously, I'd have arranged to spend it with Francie.

JUDITH. Why didn't you?

FRANK. You left it up in the air. You said you'd call me, then never did, and I've had enough of calling you and being told that you're not there. Do you realize that you've succeeded in preventing me from seeing my own daughter on Christmas Day every Christmas for the last three years?

JUDITH. I told you I'd be glad to have her here.

FRANK. The Christmas she spent with us was a nightmare!

JUDITH. I'll go right back to town!

FRANK. Sit down and have a drink, now that you're here.

She goes over and stands in front of the fireplace. He puts some ice into one of the glasses and pours in a dose of whiskey.

FRANK. You don't like soda-water, but I didn't know you were coming.

JUDITH. This is a delightful reception. You haven't even got a fire in the fireplace.

FRANK (*moving toward the door*). I'll get Bertha to bring some regular water.

JUDITH. Never mind: I'll drink it straight.

FRANK. Sure you want it that way?

JUDITH. It's all right.

He hands it to her and pours a drink for himself.

FRANK. The truth is you can't take Christmas. It always gets you down—

JUDITH. No, it doesn't.

FRANK. I don't think you've ever gotten over those perfectly grisly Christmases that you used to spend at your aunt's after your parents died—when you had to go to church in East Orange, and you said that about the only present you got was the popcorn they gave you at Sunday School.

JUDITH. You never hesitate to remind me of the unpleasant things in my life, do you?

FRANK. You remind me of them yourself—but by all means let's forget about them. (*Going over to the window-seat.*) I got you a present. I hope you'll like it, because it's something you said you wanted.

JUDITH (*looking toward the package, her childish curiosity and greediness rising to the bait*). What is it? (*As he brings it over to her, resuming her former attitude.*) You shouldn't give me a present: I didn't expect you to.

FRANK. Why not?

JUDITH. Our relations have deteriorated so. (*She un-*

ties the ribbon, opens the box and takes out the object inside.)

FRANK. Not fundamentally, perhaps.

JUDITH (*unwrapping a large jewelled comb of the kind that is supposed to be worn in Spain*). It's too big: I'd look ridiculous.

FRANK. It's just exactly what you said you wanted.

JUDITH. It's too flashy for my present style.

FRANK. Those are real emeralds.

JUDITH. Are they?

FRANK. I got them to match your eyes.

JUDITH. You should have kept it till tomorrow morning. This is only Christmas Eve.

FRANK (*giving up*). Well, you can't win: it's hopeless! It's what I told you—though you don't like to hear it: when you were little you never had a decent Christmas —so you always have to be disappointed!

JUDITH. It's not that. It's just that, under the circumstances, I don't like to have you giving me presents. (*She lays the comb back in the box and puts it on the table.*)

FRANK. But why, for God's sake?—What circumstances?

JUDITH. Oh, you know.

FRANK. You mean you've been cheating on me?

JUDITH. What you agreed to when I went to New York was really a separation.

FRANK. That wasn't *my* understanding!—Well, who's the boy-friend: Ellis?

JUDITH. I don't see Ellis any more.

FRANK (*snatching at this*). I couldn't imagine you'd find him very thrilling.

JUDITH (*with a little smile, as if to herself*). He has his points, though.

FRANK (*losing his temper*). Oh, what the hell do I care? Sleep with a different man every night! You don't need to come out here at all! You'd better keep away from me, anyway, if you want to go to any more night-clubs.

JUDITH. Is that a threat?

FRANK. No, it's not a threat: it's a statement of the simple truth! I'm just about to break the story on Luke Teniakis.

JUDITH. Right away?

FRANK. Yes.

JUDITH. In the next number?

FRANK. January 14.

JUDITH. You haven't advertised it, have you?

FRANK. Of course not. It isn't even listed in the contents.

JUDITH. I think you're crazy. He won't let it get on the stands. You remember how the Peters stopped the *New Liberal*?

FRANK. He won't find out about it.

JUDITH. He must have a spy at the press.

FRANK. It hasn't been set up at the press.

JUDITH. How are you handling it, then?

FRANK. I've set it up out here with my own hands. I learned typesetting as a kid, you know, and I got hold of an old hand-press that they were keeping as a curiosity in the local newspaper office. I bought it and set it up here in the stable. I've printed the article myself, and

I'm going to drive into town with it, and Gandy and I are going to work all night putting the pages in every copy.

JUDITH. He'll stop it right away on the newsstands.

FRANK. He won't be able to do anything about it before a lot of people have seen it. It will have gone out to all the subscribers.

JUDITH. And how will you dodge the rap?

FRANK (*exalted by desperation and by the stimulus of his drink*). I'll go up to town and live at the Plaza—

JUDITH. You better not take a room too high up!

FRANK. —I'll damn well make a point of being seen in all the most conspicuous places, and I'll just wait for the blow to fall—if they've really got the nerve to kill me. I'll go to nightclubs and shows every night—and I'm going to get a girl to go with me who'll say thank-you for Christmas presents! If they get me, maybe somebody will write on my tomb: *He died for American journalism!*

JUDITH. How did you get your facts?

FRANK. That I'm not telling anybody. But there's a damsight more dissatisfaction with Teniakis and his conspiratorial methods than you seem to realize.

JUDITH. It'll be the end of my articles! Even if *Spotlight* goes on, they'd never let me into the nightclubs. Half the nightlife in New York now is controlled by Teniakis.

FRANK. Write about something else.

JUDITH. There's nothing else that's any fun!

FRANK. Why don't you announce right away that you're resigning from the magazine?

JUDITH. I've had an offer from *Woman's World*—
Gandersheim enters.

GANDERSHEIM (*to Judith, with perceptible condescension*). Oh, hello! (*To Frank.*) The printers are on the phone.

FRANK (*nervous*). What do they want?

GANDERSHEIM. I don't know: they insisted on talking to you.

Frank goes quickly out. Gandersheim walks over to Frank's end of the table and starts checking up on the papers to make sure that nothing dangerous has been left there.

GANDERSHEIM (*to Judith*). It's nice that you could get out. We weren't certain you were coming.

JUDITH (*observing his anxiety*). Don't worry about the article: Frank's just told me about it.

GANDERSHEIM. Oh? (*Looking up at her.*) We're in your hands, then.

JUDITH. Don't worry.

GANDERSHEIM. I'm not. (*Attempting to propitiate her.*) You'll look stunning with that Spanish comb.

JUDITH. Poor Frank! He has no taste about such things.

She goes over and takes it out of the box, examining it again, to find out whether it is really expensive, whether it is really impossible for her to wear. Gandersheim, hearing the back-gate click, looks nervously out the window, sees something that arrests his attention and leans across the window-seat.

JUDITH. What do you see now, Sister Ann?—another bogeyman from Ghoul's Row?

128

GANDERSHEIM. It's Ellis.

JUDITH. No! (*She comes over quickly, with the comb in her hand, and looks out, at Gandersheim's right.*) Please don't tell him I'm here: I don't want to see him!

GANDERSHEIM. Frank will tell him.

JUDITH. Well, *you* needn't.

She goes out hastily, still carrying the comb, to shut herself up in her bedroom. Gandersheim looks after her a moment, then, coming in front of the table, moves toward the middle of the room.

GANDERSHEIM (*soliloquizing*). She's played him some dirty trick—or maybe he's found her out. He wouldn't be able to stand for her long. Such a nice clean good-looking young chap!—he had such a fine sense of decency that he wouldn't go on working for Frank when he was having a love-affair with her. That's something that's so very rare nowadays: an old-fashioned sense of honor! Our good old St. Matthew's School does really count for something still! Old Dr. Parkes at Morning Prayers and the poetry he used to read: *Say not the struggle naught availeth; Play up, play up and play the game!; Amici usque ad aras:* one always knows where one is with a person from one's own background. I had a moment of terror just now when I thought it was some stranger coming—but, thank goodness, it's only Ellis. I hope he's not still after Judy! If it's his loyalty to Frank that has brought him back, what a help he could be to us now!

Ellis appears at the door, immediately followed by Frank. Ellis has left his hat downstairs but has brought

129

with him his briefcase. Frank leaves the door partway open.

ELLIS. Hello, Gandersheim.

Gandersheim, smiling, shakes hands.

GANDERSHEIM. It seemed so delightfully natural to see you coming through the back-gate with your briefcase!

ELLIS (*to Frank*). This isn't really a social call. I want to talk business with you.

FRANK. Go on. Sit down. What's on your mind?

He sits down at the head of the table, and Ellis takes one of the chairs on the side that is nearer the audience, standing his briefcase on the table before him.

ELLIS. I'd like to talk to you alone, if you don't mind.

FRANK. Gandy sits in on all my conferences.

ELLIS. I'd rather see you entirely alone.

FRANK. That would have been all right when you were confidential secretary here—but now you're just a complainer or a favor-asker, like any other visitor. —Which are you?

ELLIS. Both.

FRANK. Shoot.

Gandersheim retires to the window-seat.

ELLIS. First of all, I'll have to explain that I'm representing an organization that I don't think you knew I was connected with: the Luke Teniakis Relief Bureau.

FRANK. I wondered what you were doing.

ELLIS. What I came to see you about is the article on the Bureau that you're planning to run.

FRANK. In the *Pressure Portraits* series? I've cancelled it.

ELLIS. I mean the other article—the one you want to bring out in this issue. (*He unfastens the briefcase, opens it and takes out a copy of the insert, leaving the briefcase, open, on the table.*)

FRANK. There isn't any other article.

ELLIS (*grinning*). I mean the one you set up in the stable—this one (*holding it up*).

FRANK. I've been seriously disappointed in you, Ellis, but I didn't expect to see you turn spy!

ELLIS (*smiling*). I'm not in the Intelligence Department. Haven't you been rather furtive yourself?

FRANK. There's nothing in the laws of the United States that says a man can't set up his own newspaper!

ELLIS. We think that a public-spirited citizen won't want to do anything on his own account that's not in the public interest.

FRANK. Who the hell is "we"? Who says what is or isn't in the public interest? I've got a damsight more right to judge that than any racketeering Greek delicatessen-dealer!

ELLIS. There's no racketeering in the Bureau. Teniakis is strict about that. The main thing, however, is that we want you to hold out the article.

FRANK. If I won't, what does your (*ironical*) organization propose to do about it?

ELLIS. What we propose to do is to explain the situation more fully, in the hope that you'll see it our way.

FRANK (*turning around toward Gandersheim*). I'll be damned: he's come out here to high-pressure me!

ELLIS. I knew you were going to say that, Frank—but

131

this is not the same thing at all as the propaganda groups who've been after you. What *we* want isn't publicity but for the press to take no notice at all of us, so that Luke can go quietly on building up the essential services. And seriously, Frank, I can tell you that the Relief Bureau *is* getting things done. The Teniakis appointees have the know-how and the know-what, as we say.

FRANK. I seem to have heard that before. I suppose you'll be telling me next that the Long Island Railroad is running on time!

ELLIS. So it is. Didn't you know? —But there's one thing that's running damn badly, and it's something that we'd like to get your help with.

FRANK. Now comes the bribe! Go on: I'm fascinated!

ELLIS. The fact is the matter came up before anybody knew about your article. The situation is that *Dopesheet* —you know *Dopesheet,* the racing journal—has got into an awful mess. McGonegal is resigning.

FRANK. Why?

ELLIS. I won't go into that now.

FRANK. I see!

ELLIS. Well, *Dopesheet* hasn't been, of course, on the very highest level of journalism, but it's always been a little more than just a racing paper. It's always stood up for the Common Man—

FRANK. And encouraged him to throw away his money. —Go on: I wouldn't miss a word of this!

ELLIS. It has real possibilities, Frank—and Luke himself has had the idea that you'd be just the man to remake it— (As *Frank seems about to explode.*) Don't answer till you've thought about it. It's more interesting than you—

FRANK. Listen, Ellis: what interests *me* is to know how a guy like you who's been brought up as a perfect gentleman can be hypnotized into falling for this mug. I'm not exactly surprised, because you can't be surprised by anything nowadays—

GANDERSHEIM. I am: I'm absolutely shocked!

FRANK. —But I feel a certain curiosity as to precisely how the feat was accomplished.

GANDERSHEIM. The man is an illiterate gangster!

ELLIS. We call him the greatest Greek since Pericles and the greatest American since Andrew Jackson.

FRANK. Why Andrew Jackson, for goodness' sake?

Judith appears in the doorway and stands listening behind the door.

ELLIS. Jackson was an early example of the Teniakis principle of Rule by the Uncommon Man in the Interests of the Common Man.

GANDERSHEIM. What would Dr. Parkes have said if he'd heard you compare Teniakis with Pericles?

ELLIS. Something very stuffy, no doubt. You have an exaggerated respect for St. Matthew's, Gandersheim— probably because you didn't finish there. If you'd been through the whole mill as I was, with Princeton and Oxford on top of it, it wouldn't have very much glamor for you. I dare say those places meant something in the fairly remote past, when they trained what were known as "the better people." Even as late as my father's day, it was possible to cherish the illusion that there still existed a world in which social distinction and scholarship and the practice of the more serious professions had some kind of real importance. But by the time *I* went to St. Matthew's, the headmaster was merely a money-raiser who had memorized a few lines from Wordsworth, and the fathers of most of the boys were nothing much more than money-raisers either—people who thought they ought to be rich but who'd been driven to desperation by the Government's inroads on business. When the parents—who were invariably divorced—came up to see the boys for weekends, they were usually as jumpy as kangaroos from having had to skip an evening's drinking.

GANDERSHEIM. There is still such a thing as a gentleman!

ELLIS. Where? There's no class of gentlemen now that counts. The ideal of public service that was a part of the upper-class tradition is only kept alive today by the fruit-dealer Teniakis, who was trained in the Greek Resistance—and if somebody like me who's been trained in those obsolete schools of conformity can help to make Luke's contacts smoother by a little St. Matthew's suavity, I'll consider that my education has not been entirely wasted. (*To Frank.*) Does that answer your question?

FRANK. It answers my question, old bean, with a frankness I'd hardly expected. And now I'm going to ask you another: What does your public-spirited leader propose to do if I fail to be won by your suavity?

ELLIS. I'll answer that question frankly, too: the article won't be distributed.

FRANK (*springing up from his chair*). By God, they can't prevent me from talking, if it's the last thing I ever do!

ELLIS. Don't kid yourself, Frank—and don't do anything foolish. I've come as a friend, believe it or—

FRANK. I anticipated something like this, and I know what to do about it. Go back and tell that clever Greek louse who's taken you on as an errand-boy that your mission was completely fruitless.

Judith comes in from behind the door, but walks around the end of the table, so as to pass on the opposite side from Ellis.

ELLIS. Don't you think that your language is rather strong for the weakness of your position? We've taken our precautions, too—

JUDITH. Hello, Ellis: what an exciting surprise! Is this a Christmas visit?

ELLIS (*looking around and rising, but greeting her rather stiffly*). Hello: I didn't know you were here.

He shakes hands with her across the table, and while this is going on, Judith, with her free left hand, quickly picks up the unfastened briefcase and, stepping back from the table and holding the briefcase away to the right, pulls out of it a large flashlight.

ELLIS (*rising and putting out his hand*). Please don't fool with that: it's broken.

She whisks it away and darts over between Frank and the window-seat.

ELLIS (*moving toward her end of the table*). Look out: it may give you a shock!

JUDITH (*to Frank*). Don't let him get it back—it's the thing they kill people with!

Frank pulls out his revolver and, stepping behind the table, stops Ellis at about halfway its length. Gandersheim has jumped to his feet and stands behind Frank. Judith gets as far away as possible, at the extreme right of the stage, with the table between her and Ellis.

ELLIS. Don't be silly! It's just a broken flashlight.

JUDITH. I know what it is! (*Examining it.*) It's one of Teniakis' distress-guns.

ELLIS. You'd better leave it alone!

JUDITH. Nonsense: I know how it works. It isn't even set to go off.—Well, a fine knight-in-armor *you* turned out to be!

ELLIS. I didn't know you were out here. You were supposed to be in town today.

JUDITH. So you came here to kill Frank!

ELLIS. I came out to try to prevent it.

JUDITH (*to Frank, holding up the flashlight*). Do you know what this really is? It's the thing they used to kill Cardinal Keenan.

FRANK. What is it?

JUDITH. It's a kind of gun. I don't understand what it shoots—that's still a military secret that only the Teniakists know. But it's something—a ray or a gas or something—that practically incinerates people.

GANDERSHEIM (*to Frank*). You remember I suggested a blow-torch?

FRANK. Hadn't we better get rid of it right away?

JUDITH. It can't go off now.

FRANK (*to Gandersheim*). See if the gardener's still out there.

GANDERSHEIM (*looking out the window*). Yes.

FRANK. Call him in.

Gandersheim knocks on the glass and gestures to the Gardener to come up.

FRANK (*to Judith, in a surly tone*). How do *you* know so much about it?

JUDITH. Somebody explained it to me.

FRANK. Who did?

JUDITH. I wouldn't want to tell.

ELLIS. *We* know, though.

JUDITH. No, you don't.

Frank, still covering Ellis, opens with his left hand a drawer in the end of the table and takes out another revolver.

ELLIS. If you care about saving your friend, you'd better give back that gun. You know I couldn't use it now, even if I wanted to.

She shoots him an ironical look.

FRANK (*to Ellis*). Well, this is a hot one! I send you up to town as a tried and trusted henchman to investigate a murder and you come back with the murderer's weapon, all ready to roast me to a cinder!

ELLIS. I'm sorry, Frank: I was trying to save you. They'd have simply bumped you off before now if I hadn't volunteered to come out here.

FRANK. You didn't come exactly unarmed!

ELLIS. It's the most humane way: I didn't want them to do any of the other things.

FRANK. I see.—May I ask, by the way, why that thing should be called a "distress-gun"?

JUDITH. It's an attempt to make these killings sound humane. The idea is that the victim is being put out of his misery. The smart trick about it is that it's set off by the emotion of the victim. It works something like radar.

FRANK. What do you mean exactly?

JUDITH. Well, you remember that article you ran about the brain producing electricity when the organs of sense were stimulated?

FRANK. Yes.

JUDITH. Well, you remember it said that pain gave comparatively faint results, and that nobody knew why this was.

The Gardener quietly enters, but does not advance into the room and is not at first noticed by Frank, who is attentively listening to Judith.

FRANK. There were dark hints about researches that couldn't be published yet.

JUDITH. You'll see why. The point was, it seems, that up to a few years ago the brain research people had only been able to study animals or patients under anesthetics who were having brain operations. But lately, in some jail in Europe that was crammed with political prisoners, they began just exposing their brains and testing their pain reactions.

FRANK. Where was this?

JUDITH. It's a secret which country did it, but the U. S. has got the technique. They know now how to use the emotions to generate electric charges, and they went the

138

Nazis one better. Instead of just making soap and lamp-shades out of human fat and skin, they amused themselves by fixing up the prison-cells with electrodes and amplifiers and having the prisoners electrocute themselves by their purely subjective emotions. They'd threaten them or disappoint them, and the electrical machine would do the rest.

THE GARDENER (*crossing himself*). *Bozhe moy!*

FRANK (*noticing the Gardener and speaking to him*). Mr. Ellis, I'm sorry to say, is no longer in sympathy with us. He's come back here as an agent of the gang we want to expose. (*Holding out the revolver, but not turning away from Ellis.*) Take this and stand by the door. If he should try to rush us, shoot him in the leg.

THE GARDENER (*coming forward*). Please forgive, little father. I can only help to fight with words. It is forbidden me to fight with weapons.

FRANK. Do you mean it's against your religion?

THE GARDENER. Yes, gracious little father.

FRANK. Good God, he's gone Russian on us now!—All right. (*Handing the gun to Gandersheim.*) You take it and go over there. (*Gandersheim complies, passing in front of the table.*)—Well, finish your story, Judy.—(*To Gandersheim.*) Keep an eye on the door, too.

GANDERSHEIM. I will, Frank. (*He comes forward so that he can see into the hallway.*)

FRANK (*to Judith*). You were saying that electric currents could be stimulated by unpleasant feelings.

JUDITH. Not merely *unpleasant* feelings, but they haven't got the hang of the pleasant ones, because emotions like hatred and fear and grief were the only ones they could be sure of producing. The gun only works for those. It was invented by a Teniakis guerrilla who was in prison and saw the experiments and had the idea of a gun that would be fired by an electrical signal set off by the victim himself. You put this thing in the room; you get your prospect overexcited; then you just go away and leave him. In the case of Cardinal Keenan, he'd been putting up a very tough fight against the Teniakis infiltration—so they called him up and told him that the new head of Tammany Hall was now a Teniakis agent. His secretary—who *was* a Teniakisite—had left the gun on a bookcase, and it automatically aimed and fired.

THE GARDENER (*crossing himself again*). *Spasi, Gospodi, i pomilui!*

FRANK. It seems unnecessarily complicated.

JUDITH. Well, the man who made it just loves gadgets and he's an incorrigible practical joker—and the device does have the advantage that the killer isn't there at all and that when people find the apparatus, they don't understand what it is.—That's what Ellis was counting on here. He knew how bad-tempered you were, and he came out to get you worked up and to leave you to storm and fume and eventually set off the gun.

FRANK (*to Ellis*). Offering me the editorship of *Dopesheet*, huh?

ELLIS. I'd like to say that Judith's account of all this is a very much distorted one.

FRANK. Distorting your behavior, Ellis, is the same as painting the lily. But the problem is what to do about

140

you. (*Indicating the morris-chair.*) Why don't you sit down while we talk about it. (*Ellis complies.*) Don't you want a drink?

ELLIS. No, thanks.

FRANK. Never drink while on duty, eh?

JUDITH (*to Frank*). I don't think you ought to hesitate to shoot him—if we could be sure of getting rid of the body.

FRANK. I don't like to do that. (*To Ellis.*) How would you like to give me your word of honor that you'd get out of the country and stay?

JUDITH (*sneering*). Ellis hasn't any honor—his word isn't worth a thing! He'll even lie out of a dinner engagement.

ELLIS. I'm sorry about that evening: I really did have to dine with my aunt—and I resent being told that my word is no good.

FRANK. Will you swear, if I let you go, that you'll clear out and say nothing? You won't want to face them after this failure. I'll supply the money.

GANDERSHEIM. Don't let him go, Frank: it's Shidnats!

FRANK. Oh, lay off that, Gandy!

GANDERSHEIM. He came from over there behind the house (*gesturing with the gun toward the window*), just as I knew he would! It's not the real Ellis—how could it be? It's Shidnats in Ellis's body. They've murdered the real Ellis!

JUDITH (*coming over to Gandersheim*). You'd better give *me* that gun.

GANDERSHEIM. Please leave me alone!

141

FRANK. Listen, Gandy: I admit that this sounds like one of your stories, but we've got to face a practical crisis, and I've just had the disquieting thought that there's nobody to watch the stuff in the stable. Will you check on it?—and go around the place? There's nobody down there but Bertha. If you've got a good incantation, it might be helpful to get it off.

GANDERSHEIM. Don't make fun of me, Frank!

FRANK. Give Judy the gun and go out and see if things are all right.

GANDERSHEIM. Whatever you say, Frank.

Judith takes the revolver from him, transferring the flashlight to her left hand. Gandersheim, chagrined, goes out, closing the door behind him.

FRANK. Do something with that infernal machine, Judy.

She crosses over, still covering Ellis, and puts the flashlight on the mantel, the bulb-end facing the stage.

JUDITH. The idea of thinking that Ellis is any different now than he ever was!

She returns and takes up her stand between Ellis and the door.

FRANK. What gets me is how he kept acting as though he were so goddam scrupulous.

ELLIS. You were urging me to get rid of my scruples when you wanted to find out about Keenan—and, given your objective, you were perfectly right.

FRANK. I didn't want you to commit any murders! What beats me is how you made the jump from being a minister's son to the role of professional killer!

142

ELLIS. As I told you, you're quite mistaken. My idea in coming out here—

THE GARDENER (*interrupting*). Forgive me, please—but if you will permit me, I understand this very well. I can perhaps explain better than he can. I was once assassin, too. In the old days in Russia, I was Neegeeleést. I took part in Neegeeleést conspiracy that assassinated Alexander Second—

FRANK. Well, that was legitimate, wasn't it? The old regime in Russia was rotten.

THE GARDENER. From political point of view, we thought we were doing right thing. But later I come to look at the matter from point of view of God, and I know then that we committed mortal sin. I did not throw bombs myself, but I was there when my comrades threw them. First bomb killed only Cossacks—but it was horrible to see even Cossacks die. Then the Tsar got down from his carriage to find out if anybody hurt, and I see that he is thin and old, that he is tired and sick and has many worries, that he drives in his own carriage like a prisoner, that the autocrat is less free than we are. For the first time, all of a sudden, I see that he is a man and I pity him. Not only he is always in danger, but he suffers on account of our hatred. Then second bomb is thrown—it explodes and tears off both his legs, and they carry him away to die in terrible unspeakable pain. I was student of natural science, then—I did not believe in Christian God, but I could not forget the face of Alexander Nikoláevich. Not very long after, I read the writings of Lyov Tolstóy, and I understand all

143

our sin. I see clearly that through hatred and violence it is impossible to cure evil—such methods only make more evil. Through love, and only through love, can evil be turned away.

ELLIS (*clearing his throat, a little embarrassed*). What I'm trying to explain is that I don't hate Frank. He may think I resented him when I worked here, but actually I've always liked him and—

THE GARDENER. You are convinced that world will be better off if you murder a man you like?

ELLIS. The world will be better off if it's decently run for once—and that's what we hope to accomplish. What about the millions of people who have been killed in these last two wars? If another such war can be stopped by a few quick and painless executions, we oughtn't to hesitate.

FRANK. How can you stop a war?

ELLIS. The Relief Bureau is international: we've got people all over the world.

THE GARDENER. It is against law of God to kill in war, and it is equally against law of God to kill for political reasons.

ELLIS. We prefer to say *administrative*.

FRANK. You're quibbling.

THE GARDENER. It is not important what you call it. All violent acts are crimes: they are offences against Christian teaching.

ELLIS. Don't think I haven't thought about this. As Frank says, I'm a minister's son. But my father had a fashionable Episcopal church and was a passionate Anglophile, and it was brought home to me very strongly by the time I was ten years old and we were fighting the Japs and the Germans that what you call the Christian teaching is *not* what's taught by the Christian church.

THE GARDENER. It is true that the churches preach war, but that is not precept of Christ.

ELLIS. No, but really—aside from the churches—you can find non-resistance in the Gospels, but you can also find the other thing. One of my father's most successful sermons was based on the text from Matthew, *I came not to send peace, but a sword.* That was during the first World War, and he had the congregation so excited that, after the service was over, the women stood out on the church steps and pinned white feathers on all the men who hadn't enlisted yet. What's the point of pretending we're Christians, and that Christianity means brotherly love? It's much better, it seems to me, to do such killing as we need without rancor. The way we regard it at the Bureau: it's just a clearing of the ground to build.

JUDITH. That's a principle that works both ways. Frank wants to build something, too, and he's got his own land to clear.

ELLIS. You're bitter against me, Judy, for reasons that are completely irrelevant and due to a misunderstanding.

JUDITH. It would be interesting to hear your story!

ELLIS. I'd be glad to tell you, if you'd let me.

JUDITH. Look, Frank: you're not getting anywhere. This is no time to argue theology. You can see that I really know something about the Teniakis business, and

I think it might be more useful if I could talk with Ellis alone.

FRANK. What light would that throw on your problem?

JUDITH. I can't explain now, but I swear to you it's really important.

FRANK. It's not important to *me* if Ellis stood you up on a date.

JUDITH. It's not that. Do leave us alone for just a few minutes. You can stand right outside in the hall. It's the only way I can help you.

FRANK. All right, but make it quick. I can't afford to waste much time. (*As he is walking toward the door, he takes the flashlight down from the mantel.*) I'll put this away somewhere.

JUDITH. No, leave it: it's safer here—because I know how it works. It's not set, and even when it is, there's a device that lets you know when it's going off. The flashlight bulb lights up and keeps burning for several minutes before the gun fires itself. That's how the killer knows when to leave, if he's had to stay in the room.

FRANK. I don't want you bumping off Ellis!

JUDITH. I won't—I promise.

FRANK. All right—keep between him and the door!

JUDITH. Don't worry.

FRANK. OK. (*to the Gardener*) Come along.

THE GARDENER. I obey, little father.

Frank goes out.

THE GARDENER (*following Frank, but turning and addressing the audience—he speaks now with a Jewish accent*). I haven't had a scene like this since Gorki's *The Lower Depths*—and the translation is terrible!

He goes out and shuts the door.

ELLIS. What I wanted to explain to you, first of all, is that I did have to go to my aunt's.

JUDITH. Do you expect her to leave you money?

ELLIS. No—but she's my father's only living sister, and a formidable old lady. She doesn't invite you often, and when she does, you have to go.

JUDITH. In other words, one of your aunts would always have a priority over me.

ELLIS. That's not the way I'd put it. I—

JUDITH (*interrupting him*). I resent your whole attitude toward me. You went to the most elaborate trouble not to have me meet your Southampton friends that night.

ELLIS. I thought they'd bore you to death. All they talk about is business and beaches.

JUDITH. I thought *he* looked rather sweet.

ELLIS (*grinning*). It may have been an instinct on my part not to have you meet somebody that looked sweet to you.

JUDITH. You didn't care about me that much!

ELLIS. Don't you think *I've* got some cause for complaint?

JUDITH. No.

ELLIS. You wouldn't even let me talk to you on the phone. And how about Pinky Papadopoulos?

JUDITH. I don't really like him. He's too Levantine.

147

ELLIS. He must have been pretty crazy about you to have told you about his gun.

JUDITH. That's what I wanted to talk about. I don't want him to get into trouble. I want you to promise me absolutely that you won't give Pinky away.

ELLIS. Otherwise, what?—you'll shoot me?

JUDITH. No: I don't want to shoot you.

ELLIS. Why should I promise, then?

JUDITH. Because I want you to.

ELLIS. I hope it's not really finished between us.

JUDITH. I didn't want it to be.

ELLIS. Shall I see you again?

JUDITH. If you want to.

ELLIS. You know I do. It was really your letting me down that made me join Teniakis.

JUDITH. No!

ELLIS. Yes, it was: I was terrifically upset. After all, I'd only seen you twice—and I hadn't ever known before what that kind of thing—what love could be like.

JUDITH. It was exciting in that sordid little room up above the Tokyo Club, wasn't it? I didn't tell you then, but that's the room the professional tarts use.

ELLIS. Yes: it transfigures everything, doesn't it? I couldn't get down to earth again afterwards. I couldn't bear to go on as I'd been doing, just being a polite young man and doing research for their articles.

JUDITH. Did you actually take the oath and give them the guarantee?

ELLIS. Yes.

JUDITH. What crime did they make you commit?

148

ELLIS. You're not allowed to tell.—I was desperate: I wanted to be hard, like you.

JUDITH. I'm sorry. I'll try to make it up to you.

ELLIS. Will you really?

JUDITH. The third time is always the best.

ELLIS. How do I know I can count on you this time?

She comes over and, sitting on the right arm of his chair, still holding the revolver in her hand, she puts her right arm around his neck and leans over and gives him a long kiss.

JUDITH (*lifting her head*). Does that convince you?

ELLIS. Yes.

JUDITH. You won't tell about Pinky?

ELLIS. No.

JUDITH. I'm really with you people, you know.

ELLIS. Are you really? You didn't act so just now.

JUDITH. That was just because I was sore at you.

ELLIS. Really?

JUDITH. Of course—but I'm not any more: it's very much the other way.

ELLIS. What about my mission, though?

JUDITH. Frank, you mean?

ELLIS. Yes.

JUDITH. That might come out all right. Just tell him you'll disappear. Give him your word of honor.

ELLIS. I don't quite like to do that.

JUDITH. Oh, come: we've had to change our ideas about human relations, haven't we?—since that day when you were saying to Frank that these movements put a premium on treachery.

ELLIS (*giving her a doubtful glance, suspicious of irony*). Of course: an impersonal relation can be something much more sacred and binding.

JUDITH. So go back and tell your headquarters that everything's been taken care of.

ELLIS. Can I depend on you? I noticed just now that your first instinct was to rush to Frank's protection.

JUDITH. Not really—it was just to get back at you.

ELLIS. What night, then?

JUDITH. Let's say the end of the week. With what's likely to happen here, I probably won't be free till Saturday.

ELLIS. You mean—Frank?

JUDITH. Yes.—Let's say Saturday, at the Tokyo, at eight o'clock. (*She moves away toward the door.*)

ELLIS. You won't shoot me if I get up from this chair?

JUDITH. What do you want to do?

ELLIS (*coming over to her, as she stops in front of the fireplace*). I just want to tell you this! (*He embraces her with his right arm and gives her a long kiss on the mouth, while with his left arm, without her seeing, he reaches to the mantlepiece and pushes a catch on the flashlight; then he relinquishes her, murmuring in a low lover's voice:*) Till Saturday—don't let me down!

JUDITH (*with a lover's look*). All right.—Go back over there.

He returns to the morris-chair. Judith walks to the door, while Ellis looks after her with a crooked smile.

JUDITH (*opening the door*). Come in.

Frank appears, with the Gardener, who hangs behind.

150

JUDITH (*to Frank*). He's going back and going to tell them that he's left the gun. That will give you time to get away. It wouldn't do to hold him here: they'd be right out to see what was wrong. He's given his word of honor that he won't let them know the real situation. Now, don't ask me how I did it—but I've got plenty on Teniakis.—Here, take this. (*She gives him the revolver and hurries out the door.*)

FRANK (*looking at Ellis intently*). Do you agree to that?

ELLIS. Yes.

FRANK. All right: be on your way! (*To the Gardener.*) See him off the place. (*To Ellis, as the latter stands up.*) I'm not even going to follow you with a gun. You've given me your word and I trust you.

ELLIS. This doesn't mean, Frank, you know, that you'll be free to distribute your article. I wish you'd come around and discuss it. Teniakis himself will talk to you. You don't understand his point of view at all—you've written about him exactly as if he were just an old-fashioned boss.

FRANK. The old-time political bosses contented themselves with stuffing the ballot—and sometimes having somebody beaten up. They didn't kidnap and murder people. And everybody knew who they were.

ELLIS. There never was a human society that didn't depend on force. We shoot our traitors and spies.

FRANK. Only in time of war—and the people gave our government that power. Who's appointed Teniakis to be judge and executioner?

ELLIS. The people are finding it pays to put things in the Bureau's hands. They're conceding—

FRANK. Well, here's one person who isn't! (*The bulb of the flashlight lights up with a sharp but unobtrusive blue light.*) Now, go on!—(*Turning to the Gardener, which gives Ellis a chance to glance toward the flashlight.*) See him out by the back and lock the gate. I'll watch from the window.

ELLIS. Good-by, Frank.

FRANK. Good-by.

Ellis goes out with the Gardener, the Gardener shutting the door. Frank puts the revolver on the table and stands thinking, his hands on his hips. Judith enters. She is very pale. She is wearing the Spanish comb and carrying a small Christmas package, done up with a rosette of ribbon.

JUDITH. You'd better get away somewhere, Frank.

FRANK (*turning around*). Get away? For God's sake, I've been prepared for this! I've got a plane on call out here, and I'm going to fly over Manhattan and as many other places as my leaflets last and bomb them with the truth about Teniakis.

JUDITH. You're not!

FRANK. I certainly am!—and maybe you'd better come along.

JUDITH. They'll get you as soon as you land.

FRANK. I'm going to land in Canada, where they've only got Commonwealth Socialism.—(*grinning*) You look wonderful with that comb.

JUDITH. I like it. I'm going to wear it. (*Awkwardly presenting her package.*) I brought you a little present.

FRANK. No! You don't mean to say! (*He takes it and unties the ribbon.*) I thought you were done with Christmas.

JUDITH. I wouldn't let Christmas go by without giving you a present.

He unrolls a gray cloth, on which are fastened a variety of enormous gold-plated tie-clips in the shape of daggers, swords and arrows. The flashlight bulb goes out.

FRANK. Tie-clips, by God!

JUDITH. You were complaining you couldn't find them anywhere.

FRANK. A completely new model, by gracious! What is this? A dagger?—an arrow—a sword! (*He detaches the dagger and clips it on his tie.*) I'm delighted!—I never feel right without one, and I haven't had a decent one for years. Baby darling! (*He kisses her.*) This makes me feel a lot better about meeting my Maker, if I've got to. I'll at least be correctly dressed.

JUDITH. You know I'm really for you, don't you?

FRANK (*with a light touch*). There are moments when my faith in you wavers.

JUDITH. But I am—I almost always am!—Oh, everything's so horrible, isn't it? You can't live with it! Let's go to Canada! I can't stand it any longer! I hate those nightclubs and places: they cheapen you—it's all so dirty! They tried to make me talk about *Spotlight*—but I wouldn't tell them a thing.

FRANK. You must have gone pretty far with somebody to get all that information.

JUDITH (*beginning to cry*). Oh, don't!—don't reproach me: I can't stand it!—I've always been loyal to you, really. That snobby little punk Ellis!—now that he's gone bad, he's more of a prig than ever. (*Sobbing and gasping.*) You know how I bought him off? I let him think that if he'd do what I asked, I'd set the flashlight for you. (*She begins to laugh and choke hysterically. The flashlight bulb goes on.*) Oh, don't look so hurt! Don't! (*As he gazes at her surprised, with a touch of alarm.*)—I can't bear to have you look hurt! I know that I've treated you rottenly, but I'll try to make up for it now. I'll go up in the plane with you—it's terribly exciting—you're the only one who's really got guts! (*She throws herself against him, clinging with her hands to his shoulders. He puts his arms around her.*) That'll be a surprise for Ellis! (*She laughs uncontrollably again.*)—I hope they asphyxiate him, the way they do with their hopeless incompetents!

FRANK. By God, today is my greatest day!—the day of desperation and glory! There are times when the whole turn against tyranny depends on just one man who dares to speak! —And you're back with me! You're back to stay?

JUDITH (*between sobs*). If you want me.

FRANK (*pulling her to him*). You've always been my real strength!—I don't fear man, devil nor delicatessen-dealer! — (*He brings out his handkerchief and wipes her eyes.*) Now, take it easy, puss.

JUDITH. I feel terribly about what I've done to you!

FRANK. Today you wiped everything out! —Now, get yourself in hand: we've got to get going.

The flashlight bulb fades off.

JUDITH. I'm ready.

FRANK. You'll have to pack some things for Canada. I'll go get Gandy. Meet me downstairs.

JUDITH. You're not going to take *him?*

FRANK. I was going to. You don't object, do you?

JUDITH (*like a sulky tearful child*). Yes.

FRANK. I don't like to leave him here alone.

JUDITH. If *he* goes, *I'm* not going.

FRANK. He'll be disappointed—but never mind. Now go on—we've got to hurry.

JUDITH. And I might as well say right now that if I'm going to come back with you again, you've got to get rid of Gandy.

FRANK (*making for the door*). All right, all right! We'll talk about that later.

The door opens, and Gandersheim enters.

GANDERSHEIM. I came up to see what your plans were. The gardener's down there on watch.

FRANK. We'll have to go ahead with Plan Two. But Judith's going to fly with me, so you needn't come. We'll need the room in the plane for the leaflets.—But you'd better find some place to hide out that nobody but me will know.—I'm going to call the pilot now. (*to Judith*) Meet me down below!

Frank hurries out. Gandersheim stands stunned, then casts a hateful look at Judith.

GANDERSHEIM. It's nervy of you to go with Frank, but

155

are you quite sure you want to be identified with what he's trying to do?

JUDITH. Frank and I always work together.

GANDERSHEIM. That's news!

JUDITH. You'd better think about getting away. If you stay around here, they may kidnap you. If I were you, I'd go to Mexico.

GANDERSHEIM. I wouldn't desert Frank!

JUDITH. He can't have you here any more.

GANDERSHEIM. What do you mean?

JUDITH. He won't need you any more because I'm coming back here to work with him.

GANDERSHEIM. Does that come from Frank?

JUDITH. Yes.

GANDERSHEIM. I hope you won't mind if I say that I don't necessarily believe it!

JUDITH. Ask him.

GANDERSHEIM. You've made him do this!

JUDITH. Yes, I have.

GANDERSHEIM. You *bitch!*

The bulb lights up.

JUDITH. Even that old theatrical line can't make you a dramatic character.

GANDERSHEIM. It makes you a bitch.

JUDITH. It'll be enough for Frank, when he knows how you talk to me in my own house!

GANDERSHEIM. Your own house! It's *my* house, please— and I've let you play utter hob with it! Transplanting my hydrangeas and all the rest!

JUDITH. Don't give yourself away so.

GANDERSHEIM. I'm sick of your insinuations!

JUDITH. It's so obvious they're sexual symbols.

GANDERSHEIM. They obviously are to you. You can't bear to have those handsome flowers flourishing in front of the house, just because you want to castrate the men!

JUDITH. I thought they'd be more appropriate behind—for you.

GANDERSHEIM. Look here: I don't care about your billingsgate. But what's not funny—what I can't forgive—is the way that you've sold out Frank—he ought to be warned against you!

JUDITH. I saved him from Ellis today.

GANDERSHEIM. You've done nothing but try to demoralize him, to kill his faith in himself and make him fail—just because you can't stand to see men succeed. You made up to Ellis in the first place just out of perversity and vanity—you're incapable of loving anyone—I'm sure you've never even known a moment of genuine physical passion! And the result was that Ellis deserted Frank. Then *you* deserted Frank yourself. If it hadn't been for me at that time, he might never have got through this crisis—and now you're trying to come between us!

JUDITH. If it hadn't been for *me*, he'd never even have known about Teniakis.

GANDERSHEIM (*getting more and more furious*). I won't have it! I won't permit it! Frank Brock is the finest person that I've ever known in my life, and you want to spoil our friendship—when you've never done anything yourself that wasn't destructive and hateful!

JUDITH. It takes one of you sissies, doesn't it, to be really nasty to a woman!

GANDERSHEIM. A woman! What kind of a woman are *you*? I thought you didn't want to be a woman. You won't condescend to have children—you don't even care to have a husband, except for an occasional meal-ticket and to amuse yourself by torturing him on rainy days. You want to compete with the men, yet you expect them to treat you with chivalry, and what a horrid yowl you set up when anybody tries to slap you down! The relation between Frank and me is absolutely staunch and true: we have confidence in one another, and that confidence is never betrayed.

JUDITH. But Frank doesn't want *you*, he wants *me*.

GANDERSHEIM. But you really don't want *him*—you just want to feel that you can make him squirm—to titillate your own ego!

JUDITH. Now, stop that! —I won't stand for it, I tell you!

GANDERSHEIM. You know what you are? —you're Shidnats Slyme! You're not a woman at all! You're neither a man nor a woman!

JUDITH. That's an amusing accusation from you.

GANDERSHEIM. I never thought he'd come in skirts, and that's why I didn't recognize him—but that's what's so horrible, I see it now—that's what's giving the world its short circuit: the woman that won't be a woman, the woman that the men can't depend on! My mother was a thwarter, not a letter-down—but it was part of the same thing: she wouldn't let my father travel, she wouldn't send me back to school. And what good is a woman, for pity's sake, if she doesn't want to make *men*?!

JUDITH. A woman can't make a man if he hasn't got the makings of a man.

GANDERSHEIM. I was a man today all right when I had this gun in my hand (*he picks the revolver up from the table*)—when Frank and I were standing up to Teniakis!

JUDITH. No, you weren't. Put that down!

GANDERSHEIM. You're frightened of a man with a gun! —well, that's symbolical, too.

JUDITH (*showing signs of becoming hysterical*). Put it down! —put that gun away!

GANDERSHEIM. Your father and mother, eh?

JUDITH. Don't dare to talk about that!

GANDERSHEIM. I'm afraid it gives me great satisfaction to feel for just once in this house that I've got the upper hand of a woman! If my father had frightened my mother the way I'm frightening you, I might have had the romantic life I was longing for. Maybe that was the way that *your* father felt when he shot his wife and himself!

JUDITH (*shrieking before Gandersheim has finished*). —Help—oh, Frank, help!

GANDERSHEIM. All right: I'll put it away. (*He replaces the revolver on the table.*) You'd better pull yourself together if you're going to go up in that plane.

She stares at him, her mouth open, her brows contracted, in a tragic childish mask of terror. Frank comes running in. The Gardener appears behind him, but does not approach much farther than the door.

159

FRANK (*putting his arm around Judith*). What's the matter? what's going on?

JUDITH. He was threatening me!

GANDERSHEIM. That isn't true.

JUDITH. He was threatening me with the gun!

GANDERSHEIM. I wasn't.

FRANK (*to Judith*). Now, for God's sake don't have one of your fits—if you do, I can't take you with me—and we ought to leave—it's almost eight. (*He looks at the clock on the mantel.*)—My God, that thing's lit up!

They all look up at the flashlight.

GANDERSHEIM. The little blue light!—that's *it!* Shid-nats is behind that, too!

Frank quickly takes the flashlight down.

JUDITH (*completely unstrung but trying to concentrate*). Wait a minute—I know how it works. (*She fumbles at it with shaking hands.*) There's a button, but it's not the one that looks like a flashlight button—

Frank takes hold of the flashlight.

GANDERSHEIM (*in a panic*). I did this! He's in me now —he's taken possession of me!

JUDITH. Make him get out—he'll set it off!

FRANK. Better throw it out the window.

GANDERSHEIM (*to Judith, as he starts to withdraw toward the door*). You're setting it off yourself!

A blaze of blue livid light, lit up from the mantelpiece, illuminates the whole room. We see Gandersheim, Frank and Judith, for a moment, with their mouths gaping open. Then Gandersheim falls back on the table, and Frank and Judith collapse in front of the fireplace.

*The flare then quickly fades out, along with the other
lights, leaving the stage in darkness.*

*The Gardener, his figure irradiated against the opaque
black background, is revealed at the front of the stage,
in the center and facing the audience. He is standing
erect now, with an austere Hebraic head thrown back. He
speaks with the accent and the somber tones of a tragedy
in the Jewish theater.*

THE GARDENER. Like Apollo in the house of Admetus,
I must depart at the advent of death—I, Ahasuerus, the
doomed rabbi, the Wandering Jew. In many different
countries, in many different tongues, I have played your
stage gardener, your moralist. But what use for me to
continue today if my words cannot influence the action.
What use to play commentator merely in a world I can
no longer guide? We, the Children of Israel, gave you
the God of the Old Testament, and you judged and punished like him. We gave you the God of the New Testament, and you tried to forgive and love. We gave you the
Social Revolution, and you tried to judge the men of the
present and to love the men of the future. But I who
mocked at our prophet Christ, who told him to walk
quicker as he carried the cross and who therefore was sen-
tenced to wander till Christ should return again—I have
lived through two thousand years to see all these moral-
ities fail. Even Israel has forgotten its prophets—for,
goaded by the outrage and cruelty of the people of hea-
then lands who have rejected the laws of God, we have
claimed our own land again and defended it against violence with violence. No one can reproach us now for our

helplessness, our homelessness—but in that home that Israel has now regained, I no longer have any place. They will never give me a passport for Palestine. And, in your country, who will receive me?—who will recognize the sign of God? who will fight at the command of the spirit?—who will even serve the vision of Justice that has gleamed for our secular leaders? For you, God and spirit and vision are fading with the words that name them. What you trust in, for all your techniques, for all your mechanisms of industry and politics, is simply the brute vitality that animates the universe—and our own people, dwelling among you, are exchanging their traditional discipline of religious and social theory for the new one of electronics. So now you must make your new rules, develop your new calculations. They are based on statistical averages, and I cannot help you there, for my gospel has all been derived from the conscience, the courage, the insight, by which men of a chosen race asserted their superior authority. This household that, stranded and harried, has destroyed itself before our eyes seemed the only place left me for shelter—and whom can I work for now? My friends are few and weak—I have hardly even self-declared enemies to advertize God's agent by fearing him. (*The light on him begins to dim but leaves his face illumined.*) Why must I wander still? Was Jesus deceived?—will He not come again? Am I already half a wraith that flickers for a moment still in your terrorized darkness of soul when you are tortured or tempted by the forces that are pressing you into alien shapes? Is

162

the star of Bethlehem setting, on this night of the Holy Nativity, as the little blue light of hate?

Yet even in this black night of blasphemy I cannot yet die or rest: I must go on to new unbelievers. God's hand still directs and drives me—though perhaps to the last precipice-edge above which mankind must falter. God has created the Light, and the Light will not wholly fail—I shall bear it, though the Heavens be darkened, to show where the abyss drops. Now farewell—but I shall always be with you—somewhere, at some man's side!

The light on his face goes out.